Algorithmic Methods for
Artificial Intelligence

Algorithmic Methods for Artificial Intelligence

Michael Griffiths
and Carol Palissier

Chapman
and Hall

First published in 1986 by Hermes
51 rue Rennequin, 75017 Paris, France
Copyright © 1986 Hermes

English language edition first published in 1987
by Kogan Page Ltd, 120 Pentonville Road, London N1 9JN

Published in the United States of America by Chapman and Hall
29 West 35 Street, New York, N.Y. 10001

Copyright © 1987 Hermes

ISBN 0-412-01541-5 (cloth)
ISBN 0-412-01541-2 (paperback)

Printed and bound in France

Contents

Preface

This book introduces artificial intelligence to non-specialists. It is concerned with programming methods and algorithms. The aim is practical, even though abstraction is necessary. To avoid presenting the theory in depth, techniques are usually presented through examples.

The algorithmic part of the book is preceded by two independent chapters. The first, Chapter 1, recalls the origin and scope of artificial intelligence. The second, Chapter 2, resumes techniques in programming and data structures which, while presenting no particular difficulty, are often unknown to self-taught programmers.

Chapters 2 and 3 are comparatively simple. They will probably not be included in a book of this type in a few years' time, since it is reasonable to suppose that with the stabilization of curricula, this subject matter will be included in all standard university courses. The chapters which follow are more mathematical. The whole text can be considered as an apprenticeship which will allow the reader to study more advanced topics presented elsewhere.

This is the second version of the book, the limited original edition was published in French. During the process, we were helped by several colleagues, to whom thanks are due. Françoise Nayroles and Louis Bourelly helped at different points. Inspiration also came from working with a group led by Michel Maury at the University of Montpellier, and in particular from the theses of Anne-Marie Massotte and Henri Betaille.

The French magazine *Jeux et Stratégie* kindly allowed the use of published problems, for which the full references are given in the References.

A job such as this needs material support, given in the first place by our laboratory, the Groupe de Représentation et Traitement de Connaissances (GRTC) of the CNRS at Marseille. The text was prepared on computing equipment supplied by the Centre Mondial Informatique et Ressource Humaine and by the Institut International de Robotique et d'Intelligence Artificielle de Marseille (IIRIAM).

Michael Griffiths
November 1986

Figures and programs

CHAPTER 1

History and scope of artificial intelligence

Introduction
Artificial intelligence has been studied for over thirty years, first as intellectual speculation, then as an oversold set of over-ambitious projects, and finally as a respectable academic science. It has now become a subject with wide application in different fields, which is one reason for this book. We aim to make the techniques of a difficult subject available to computer users. As with all new developments which might have an impact on human life style, artificial intelligence has been the subject of controversy. It is not our aim to comment on different people's opinions, but rather to study the programming methods which are involved in its use. We believe firmly that it is up to the potential users of the technology to decide how they use it, the duty of the scientist being to explain the facts as he understands them best.

It is perhaps useful to look at the reasons behind this perturbed genesis of a discipline which is surely going to be useful in fields as far apart as computer aided design, medicine and law. The most important factor is the bringing together of the computer and the human brain. This has provoked tremendous reaction from psychologists, teachers and doctors, without mentioning the doubts of ordinary citizens. It was thought originally that computer scientists were trying to make a complete model (perhaps improved) of the human brain. This is far from true. The computer scientist tries, often with the help of an expert from a particular application field, to make a program which, given a certain number of problems, would take the same decisions as a competent human being. The decision algorithm depends on analysing the application, without necessarily following the decision process of the human brain.

In different directions, computer scientists have attacked very difficult problems, while suggesting that remarkable developments were imminent. Consider two examples from 1960. At that time, Botwinnik, the then world chess champion, who is also an electronic engineer working on computers, foresaw that a program could become the world champion ten years later. When we consider these untrue predictions made by an expert, it is easy to imagine those of less competent reviewers. In the same year were published reports on automatic translation which predicted the disappearance of human translators and interpreters in a short space of time. Such audacity raised a rapid reaction, since the aims announced not having been achieved, annual funding in the field was severely reduced. Note that, in both cases, feelings are now calm, programs exist, and they are interesting and useful, even if not perfect. The science can now proceed normally, and we may hope that the twenty-first century will see the results predicted for 1970.

To the sources of these problems should be added the corporate image of threats from the computer to reduce employment in different fields, together with the reactions of the general public, who fear a future of the type foreseen by George Orwell in *1984* (Orwell 1949).

Since feelings have calmed down, artificial intelligence can now be considered as a branch of computing like any other, which allows us to categorize some traditional application fields. Like many such classifications, the one that follows is incomplete, but will give some idea of the scope of the subject:

1) combinatorial problems, often through games, and in particular chess;
2) theorem proving and its applications;
3) automatic translation and the treatment of natural languages;
4) pattern recognition (image, speech or signals);
5) expert systems and knowledge representation, that is modelling the logic of different application fields;
6) learning and modelling cognitive processes, etc.

Note that, in each application field, computer scientists collaborate with specialists from other disciplines such as linguists, psychologists or experts in fields which are modelled. We describe the history of each category before examining the underlying programming techniques. Using these new tools is not just an act of faith, but is based on real experience in laboratories and in certain industries.

Application fields

The idea of using a computer for applications which now bear the label of artificial intelligence dates from the first published articles on computing, at the end of the Second World War, by some of the first well known names (eg Turing 1950). Scientific thinking of this type completed the vision of science fiction writers who considered social problems (Orwell 1949, Huxley 1932, Asimov 1950).

CHESS AND OTHER GAMES

General game theory together with the computing techniques behind its implementation have received much attention from research workers. A particularly important effort has gone into the game of chess, for which there exists a large number of programs.

It was one of the biggest names of his generation who wrote the first article (Shannon 1950) in which can be found the basis of current theory. A running program based on his ideas was produced by Alex Bernstein on an IBM 704 in 1958. This work has been preceded by articles written in Germany, under difficult conditions, at the end of the war (Zuse 1945), but these were only discovered twenty years later. Since these pioneering articles, there have already appeared over 300 English language articles (Marsland 1979), without mention of those written in other languages (Meissenberg 1968).

During the 1950s and early 1960s, the first programs, experimental and general, imposed evaluation principles which worked on trees as their principal data structure. We see later some tree manipulation techniques, together with strategies such as the alpha-beta algorithm or minimax. The level of play of these programs was average, and it would not have been possible to enter them in competitions. Even those programs which played relatively well were easily beaten by a human player with good strategical judgement.

Once the general evaluation method is established, it becomes necessary to improve programs by including specific knowledge, just like a player who studies, for example, end game strategy with king and pawns against king. End game analysis by computer has been used in international competitions by Russian grandmasters during adjournments, which reflects the quality of certain programs. At this level of chess, computers have not been shown to be useful in openings, nor in middle game play.

The progress of general programs is such that there came into being, in the 1970s, national chess tournaments for computers (Newborn 1972, Souls and Marsland 1975, Richter 1976), and even world championships (Mittman 1974), of which the first was won by Kaissa, a Russian program. The references are to the first championship in each case. Such championships are now producing interesting games, and programs are often accepted in tournaments together with, and under the same rules as, human competitors, with acceptable results.

The best illustration of the current quality of chess playing programs is perhaps the availability on the market, over the past few years, of programs running on microcomputers which are useful for chess players in providing them with a suitable opponent who is always available. A computer has not yet won the world championship, but programs already play better than most human players below national level. Starting from the current situation, game analysis and knowledge implementation are sufficiently difficult to make progress relatively slow, and estimations of the date at which a program will be world champion get further away every year. For state of the art programs read Clarke (1977, 1980).

While research into chess has dominated, other games should not be forgotten. Samuels (1959) is a fundamental article which considered checkers, the American form of draughts. Another important step was the resolution, by learning, of the game of GO-MOKU, a Japanese form of noughts and crosses (TIC-TAC-TOE) which needs five pieces in a row on a 19*19 board (Elcock and Murray 1967). As far as the author knows, this was the first program which played better than human beings in a serious game. Another achievement was the win by a program (The Moor), on June 19th, 1980, at REVERSI/OTHELLO, against the world champion Hiroshi Inoue. The same accident happened to the world backgammon champion at around the same time.

The state of the art programming of a set of games, with

implementation indications, can be found in a very readable book by Levy (1983).

THEOREM PROVING

During the early days of the 1950s and 1960s, the automation of reasoning was one of the ideas of computer scientists which would show that the computer could do things which were considered to be the monopoly of human beings. Producing proofs of theorems was a philosophical challenge as well as a scientific one.

It is once again striking that the first efforts were very early on. In 1954 the first steps were made, using low power computers. Davis (1957) describes a program which proved that the sum of two even numbers is even. While this result is of limited importance, those produced by the system of Newell *et al.* (1957) are more impressive. This group proved all the theorems of part of *Principia Mathematica* (Whitehead and Russell 1910), which constitutes a privileged domain for the kind of logic involved. The principles they established still hold, proofs being represented by traversals across the ramifications of derivation trees.

The mechanization of theorem proving was able to start early on in computing because it followed a well-established mathematical line of study. Davis (1983) contains a description of the important steps in mathematical reasoning, starting with Descartes. The list of names of mathematicians who contributed reads like an honours board of two centuries of mathematics.

Even if theorem proving had remained simply an intellectual challenge, it would already have provided material for interesting scientific reflection. But it has become still more important for the evolution of programming methodology. In addition, a theorem prover is an essential part of an expert system, as will be seen on page 21 and in Chapter 5 which describes them more fully. It is thus now an essential component of the modern applications of computing. All future computer aided systems will use such methods. The two directions (programming methodology and inference engines) have been followed relatively independently.

It took more than fifteen years for computer scientists to realize that writing a program is analogous to proving a theorem, since it takes a starting hypothesis (conditions on the input data), and applies transformations, described by the program, to obtain an arrival hypothesis (the required result). The proof of the correctness of a program is that of the equivalence of two formulations, the external specification and its implementation as a program text. Mechanizing such proofs runs into several difficulties. Two texts are required, the validity of a specification can be doubted, and proofs are long and complicated. But this research has thrown new light on programming methodology, and has influenced traditional methods, whether in teaching or in industry. It is not necessary to share the rampant enthusiasm for buzz-words such as 'structured programming' to realize that the underlying phenomenon is real, and has improved the output of a generation of programmers, both qualitatively and quantitively. At the same time, programming languages have benefited from formal definitions such as, for example, the axiomatic approach of Hoare and Wirth (1972).

In expert systems, theorem provers are directly used to do the necessary logical calculations. In a given situation, possible hypotheses are presented to the system as theorems, to be demonstrated or refuted. The inference engine is thus heavily used. These problems are the subject of Chapters 4 and 5.

NATURAL LANGUAGE

Automatic translation was one of the challenges of the glorious years. It was here also that the ups and downs of financial support were the most marked. In the early 1960s, it was suggested that translators and interpreters would be a dying race; in the 1970s, automatic translation was an impossible dream. It is now a normal research topic, with useful products which nevertheless leave space for improvement.

The idea of automatic translation dates to ten years before the over-optimistic predictions. In 1949, Yngve and Bar-Hillel were already working on a system at MIT (Yngve 1961). During the 1950s, experiments were carried out in both the United States and the Soviet Union which led to operational systems. There were even discussions on the possibility of international standardization of certain aspects (Kent 1961).

The systems of the 1960s having shown up the limitations of the then available techniques, many research groups were disbanded. With the reconstruction of the 1970s progress in linguistics and in computing, and the reformulation of aims and ambitions, work is now proceeding on a more solid base. The dream of a perfect system is no longer in fashion, but, as for chess playing programs, useful products are being produced.

Natural language treatment by computer is not limited to automatic translation. To simplify access to computers by non-specialist users, interfaces are needed which do not require any paricular technical knowledge to use them. The most obvious solution is to understand the user's natural language, even though this requires considerable computer power. Natural language interfaces agreeably complement the technique of menus in dialogue systems, as for example in Bobrow *et al.* (1977), which handles air timetables. To limit the amount of work done by the computer, and to stay within the state of the art, such systems often consider subsets of languages, such as Colmérauer (1981) for French.

A first use of English as an interface is to be found in McCarthy (1958), as a component of a larger project. Weizenbaum (1966) describes a simple program called Eliza which appears to carry out a conversation. In fact, Eliza replies to remarks by transforming them. Rising to the next level of comprehension is altogether more difficult, and research is particularly active. Rosenberg (1980) gives an idea of the situation as it was at the end of the 1970s.

Computer scientists consider that their research on natural language has provoked important changes in linguistics. It is certainly true that the existence of the computer, with its capacity to store and use formal grammars, has led to a new look at the work of grammarians. This encouraged the creation of formal grammars for languages, such as Salkoff (1973), which have a solid mathematical foundation. Amongst those who have influenced scientists in this direction, Chomsky has a special place. In Chomsky (1965) he analyses the deep structure of English. His work is used by linguists and computer scientists alike, and we can but regret that the two disciplines have not followed this example of a common spirit.

PATTERN RECOGNITION

Pattern recognition is an important part of artificial intelligence, with a large number of applications appearing on the market. Amongst these are speech recognition for the control of machines, identification of objects by an electronic eye to facilitate their manipulation by robot, sorting cell samples to diagnose different diseases, optical character recognition to save typing of texts or the identification of the 'signature' of a submarine, ie its identification from emitted waves.

There are two possible approaches to the pattern recognition problem. One has its origin in mathematics, the other in computing. Signal analysis has been much studied by applied mathematicians, in particular in the field of radar. The algorithmic approach of computer scientists is rather different. It is often based on the syntactic description of objects which are to be recognized. The complete process requires both types of technique. Numerical treatment is particularly useful during the first stage of object identification. It uses filters, and other statistical methods, which allow, for example, the recognition of the limits of objects in a scene, the elimination of light reflection effects (points of brilliance), the identification of phonemes in speech (with possible alternatives) or the positioning of hidden lines in an image.

The algorithmic approach is useful in finding the relationships between objects. It allows the resolution of problems such as the reconstitution and the comprehension of a phrase made up of recognized phonemes, the interpretation of an image photographed from a satellite to evaluate the agricultural production of a country, the discrimination of healthy from cancerous cells in a picture in which cell frontiers are already indicated, and so on.

It is not possible to resume such a large quantity of work in a few pages. In order to evaluate the state of the art, conferences such as IEEE are useful. Note that these publications follow a line which had a thirty year history (see, for example Davis *et al.* 1953, Fry and Denis 1953, Baumann and Licklide 1954).

It can be asked whether the last thirty years' work have led to useful and concrete results. The reply is necessarily ambiguous. Pattern recognition, like the rest of artificial intelligence, has turned out to be difficult, and expensive in terms of computer requirements. This latter factor is particularly important in pattern recognition, which models a human activity which is based on parallel methods on a computer which is essentially still sequential.

So the success rate of pattern recognition systems is variable. Optical reading is operational for printed texts, or even typed ones, under the condition of carefully adjusting input parameters to the set of characters to be read. Manuscript is essentially unreadable, although it may be possible to identify the author. For speech recognition, industrial systems exist which work well with small vocabularies spoken carefully so as to separate the words. They usually require an apprenticeship, which is a learning program which allows the system to get used to each new speaker. It may be that continuous speech recognition, with multiple speakers, while not yet being available, is a reasonable goal. Speech synthesis is already with us on an industrial level. Automatic picture analysis has been particularly stimulated by the arrival in laboratories of images taken by cameras onboard satellites. However, work in this field is not yet definitive. At a practical level, success has been achieved in scanning medical images, for example in separating cell samples into healthy samples, cancerous ones, and undecided. Such systems are operational, and have notably diminished the frequency of human intervention.

To resume, pattern recognition, while being part of artificial intelligence, is a subject too vast to be covered in a general presentation. Interested readers ought to consult the specialized literature, since the subject will not be further studied in this book.

EXPERT SYSTEMS AND KNOWLEDGE
Compared with other branches of artificial intelligence, expert systems are relatively new. They appeared first in the 1960s, and the term came into general use at the end of the 1970s. However, current fashion means that everybody is now using the term.

In a system of this type, it is hoped to provide answers to questions asked in the scope of a given application field. Replies should be as good as those supplied by a human expert. To do this, the system contains a set of deduction rules. It applies these to a set of facts, modelling human reasoning, usually by means of a theorem prover.

The best known applications of expert systems are in medicine, starting with MYCIN (Shortliffe 1976). Other applications which have been useful in practice are R1, a system to reconfigure VAX computers by DEC (McDermott 1982), and Prospector, a system which helps geologists to find mineral deposits (Duda *et al.* 1979). Several hundred systems have since appeared, but most of them are at the level of experimentation or pilot projects. We are just on the verge of industrial implementation on a large scale.

At the current time, there exists a large number of theorem provers which are used as inference engines for expert systems. There has even been a certain unbalance between research and development, since more effort has gone into theorem proving than into applications. The most difficult problems in expert systems are the analyses of fields of expertise but the situation is improving.

Transforming expert knowledge into information described in a form acceptable to a computer requires someone capable of analysing completely his field of work. The job is difficult and painstaking, and necessitates collaboration between computer scientists and particularly competent users. A new profession is emerging, that of knowledge engineering. For a project to succeed, it is not sufficient to accumulate the necessary information; severe problems arise in its representation, storage and manipulation.

LEARNING

Learning is the process through which a human being or a program profits from experience. Trials are made. They are catalogued following the degree of satisfaction obtained. As in the case of other techniques, the first programs concerned games.

The early checkers program already cited (Samuels 1959) kept a catalogue of all the positions it encountered. Note also that, in order to find played positions rapidly, Samuels was the first user of hash coding. During this period of time, IBM also had several learning projects under way (Freidberg 1958, 1959).

After these projects, which explored methods of cataloguing examined positions, others went on to the evaluation of experiments. In Michie (1962) occurs the idea of rewarding a position which led to a win at TIC-TAC-TOE, and punishing a losing one. Reward and punishment increase or decrease the probability of making a move which leads to the position. In the experiment quoted, it only required 200 games for the system to learn to win each time this was possible. We should also not forget the achievement of Elcock and Murray (1967), whose program for GO-MOKU overtook human capabilities by using a learning algorithm.

Learning is now integrated into the techniques used in

different fields, such as chess playing programs, optical readers or speech recognition. In chess, it is used to optimize the values of parameters used for the evaluation of positions, such as the value of pieces, the importance of control of the centre, etc. In pattern recognition, it allows the program to adjust itself to the input data. In speech recognition the different speakers give the system examples of a known representative vocabulary in order to establish their particular wave patterns (see, for example Gerard and Mercier 1981). In the same way, an optical reader 'learns' the physical characteristics of the text to be read, such as type fount and spacing. Other applications are to be found in the field of computer aided learning.

Techniques and tools in artificial intelligence
One of the difficulties in writing this book is that the term artificial intelligence is in fact not defined. In general, it is identified with the work done by those members of the computing community who use the term. Their characteristics are those of attacking a set of problems which have the reputation of being too difficult, and using programming methods thought to be advanced, marginal or inefficient. These differences in comparison with the rest of computing are perhaps less marked nowadays, but this has not lessened the feeling of belonging to a special group.

The first research groups, faced with problems to which they could not find determinist solutions, adopted a specific style and language, for example in using recursion systematically. The advantages of a recursive style in programming are multiple. In the first place, there is a direct link with recurrence (induction), and it is by recurrence that it is often useful to attack algorithmic problems. What is more, recursion leads to programs which are compact and readable, properties which are needed in order to dominate program complexity. A lot of nonsense is talked about efficiency in computing, but if it is important, and if recursion is one of the causes of inefficiency in a given situation, we now have satisfactory tools to transform recursive programs into iterative form.

Recursion in programs corresponds to the recursive structure of artificial intelligence data. It is on structures such as trees and graphs that we represent abstractions of the real world. Since these objects are recursively defined, it is natural that the programs which manipulate them are written in a

23

form which follows the data. The same is true for the symbolic representation of objects, since loogical formulae allow unlimited nesting, and hence contain intrinsic recursion.

Symbolic representation of situations by logical formulae is a part of artificial intelligence which makes use of mathematical logic. While first order logic remains the most important, other forms are studied and used in theorem provers. The kind of programming which is of interest here requires competence in logical algebraic manipulation. Chang and Lee (1979) is a useful book which approaches logic from the point of view of the computer scientist.

In addition to a particular programming style, particular methods of solution are also necessary, such as backtracking, heuristics, evaluation by minimax or alpha-beta, pattern directed inference, and numerical or statistical methods used in pattern recognition and signal analysis. Some specific resolution methods constitute Chapter 3.

Given the specificity of style and method, it is not surprising to discover that there exist specific languages for artificial intelligence. The first of these is LISP (McCarthy 1960, 1978). There have been thousands of implementations, and hundreds of variants, dialects and successors of this language, which represents one of the important steps in the history of computing. LISP has influenced the thinking of generations of programmers.

More recently, a second language, **PROLOG** (Roussel 1975), has become popular by large scale use, the number of implementations and copies, and the abundance of literature on it. LISP and **PROLOG** are distinguished from the hundreds of other languages for artificial intelligence in that they are the only ones universally known to specialists all over the world. Their importance is such that Chapter 6 is devoted to them. For other given programs, a more standard language is used. A resume of it is to be found in Appendix 1.

CHAPTER 2

Data structures and program structures

Artificial intelligence programs employ advanced programming techniques. Some of them, but not all, contain real intellectual difficulties. Trying to indicate the characteristics of these programs can lead to the following, incomplete list:

1) complex data structures;
2) programs which are often recursive;
3) non-numerical calculations;
4) long execution time;
5) a large number of cases to consider;
6) difficult algorithmic problems;
7) specific programming techniques;
8) specific languages, usually non-traditional.

In this chapter are considered those data structures that are often encountered, together with the corresponding program structures. Readers who have used manipulating trees or graphs, and who have already written heavily recursive programs, will find themselves in familiar territory.

The programming language used
The programs which occur in the early chapters of this book are written in an algorithmic language which resembles PASCAL but there are a few differences, due to the fact that a book is for human communication only, and that there is no need to satisfy a compiler. The programs will need some small amount of rewriting to run on a computer.

In particular, keywords (BEGIN, IF, ...) are in capital letters, identifiers in lower case. Not all declarations are given. Of course, those that are included follow the syntax of PASCAL. In general, the programs to initialize arrays and other variables are left to the reader. Conditional structures are completely bracketed by IF-THEN-ELSE-FI or IF-THEN-FI, which reduces the need for BEGIN-END pairs. The CASE construction can be an expression or an instruction. Comments start with two dashes -- and continue to the end of the line (as in ADA). The Boolean operators CAND and COR order tests in expression evaluation, and avoid the evaluation of potentially dangerous, and useless, subexpressions. A resume of the language is included in Appendix 1.

Trees

Consider the problem of writing a chess playing program. In a given position, the program looks for the best move for its side. To do this, it examines the set of available moves. For each move it looks at possible replies, to which there are new reply sets, and so on up to a certain number of moves in advance. The positions to be examined can be represented in the form of a tree, as shown in Figure 1.

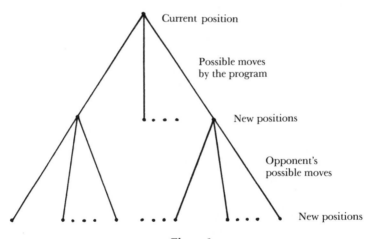

Current position

Possible moves
by the program

New positions

Opponent's
possible moves

New positions

Figure 1.
Position tree for chess

Note that this structure already illustrates several of the characteristics given at the beginning of this chapter. In particular, given the large number of possible moves in any chess position, the number of cases quickly becomes enormous (about a million after four moves).

Trees are not only useful for programming games. A whole

series of problems needs the same kind of structure. For example, in order to calculate the trajectory of an automatic tender in a cluttered workshop, each possible movement of the tender can be considered as a position on a tree. Different displacements reduce to the traversal of the representation tree (or graph). Trees are used each time that, in a given situation, different possibilities are available. Numerous other examples are given in this book.

A tree is a structure with an origin, its root. The root is a particular member of the set of nodes. Each node has its specific value (or set of values), together with a set of successors. In the example of the chess playing program, the root is the current position. Its successors are the positions which would result from each possible move. Obviously, each successor has its own successors, which are those positions resulting from possible replies, and so on. The value attached to each node is the appropriate position on the chessboard.

A node with no successor is called a leaf. The existence of leaves means that trees can be finite. Computer scientists have adopted the unfortunate convention which draws trees upside down, that is with the root at the top and the leaves at the bottom. A traversal from root to leaf is called descending or top-down, and from leaf to root ascending or bottom-up.

The trees in this book are all cleanly constructed, that is that each node is the successor of one and only one node. The root is unique, and is distinguished by the fact of being the only node with no predecessor. Thus, branches of trees do not rejoin, and there are no loops. Extending trees to allow paths to rejoin leads to lattices, whereas allowing loops leads to graphs.

Trees have been widely studied in the literature, and are taught in standard computer science curricula. There are expository texts available, such as Knuth (1968) which can be read by non-specialists.

Tree traversal
The classic tree traversal program is a recursive procedure which, for each node encountered, visits each of its successors. It is given as Program 1.

```
PROCEDURE visit(node);
    -- prefix functions
    FOR each_successor(node)
    DO visit(successor)
    DONE;
    -- postfix functions
END visit;
```

Program 1.
Tree traversal

The traversal is initiated by a call of the procedure with the root as parameter:

visit (root);

During each tree traversal, the same function is frequently applied to each node. A node may be treated before or after its successors, that is to say in prefixed or postfixed order. For each of these the function is inserted at the place of the relevant comment in the procedure of Program 1.

Tree representation

Languages used for this kind of programming often supply a means of expression which allows the direct representation of trees. But even in this favourable situation, possibilities are usually limited to trees with a fixed number of successors per node. It is for reasons of this type that we usually allow only binary trees, which are trees which have at most two successors to each node.

This limitation can appear to be too severe, since it is obvious that, in any position of chess, there are many more than two possible moves. In fact, it is not a problem, since any n-ary tree may be transformed into a binary tree without loss of generality. It is simply necessary to put the tree 'on its side', as in the following example, in which the tree is put into the form called a vine diagram.

In an n-ary tree, a node is a record of the following type:

(value, succ1, succ2, ...)

It is transformed into the following record:

(value, first-succ, follower)

Figure 2 gives a tree with three successors per node, which is transformed, in Figure 3, into a binary tree.

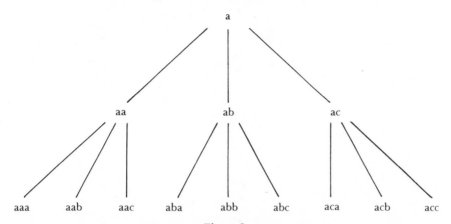

Figure 2.
Tree with three successors per node

Note that Figure 3 gives the complete tree. When there is no successor, this is indicated by an arc towards the nil element X. Since the transformation always exists, we only consider binary trees in the rest of this book.

Representing binary trees is simple, whatever programming language is used. Consider nodes with integer values. The tree can be represented in a table with three columns, which contain the value, the left successor and the right successor. There exists an equivalance between a row of the table and the triplet which represents a node:

(value, left-successor, right-successor)

A node is identified by its position in the matrix (the index of its row). Successor column entries contain the indices of the relevant nodes. A non-existent successor is signalled by the NUL element in the appropriate entry. Figure 4 shows the translation of Figure 3 into table form, in which the node values are their names.

In this table, the nil element is represented by -1, a suitable integer. Since the matrix is indexed from 1 to n, -1 cannot be an index. Left or right successors are found by using the corresponding entry (Lsucc or Rsucc) as an index.

To be complete, Program 2 gives the form of the procedure visit for the case of a binary tree.

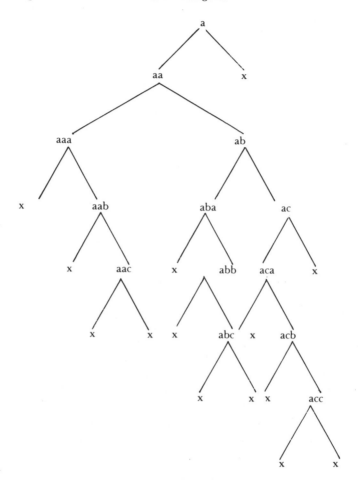

Figure 3.
Equivalent binary tree

This form of the procedure has the advantage of allowing the three standard traversals, prefixed, infixed and postfixed of a binary tree. These terms come from the use of trees to represent and evaluate arithmetic expressions. The test assumes the existence of a procedure which knows when a given successor exists. With the table representation of Figure 4, the test of existence is a comparison with -1.

Graphs

Intuitively, graphs can be considered as extensions of trees.

Index	Name	Lsucc	Rsucc
1	a	2	-1
2	aa	5	3
3	ab	8	4
4	ac	11	-1
5	aaa	-1	6
6	aab	-1	7
7	aac	-1	-1
8	aba	-1	9
9	abb	-1	10
10	abc	-1	-1
11	aca	-1	12
12	acb	-1	13
13	acc	-1	-1

Figure 4.
Binary tree represented by a matrix

```
PROCEDURE visit(node);
      -- prefixed function
      IF exists(left(node))
      THEN visit(left(node))
      FI;
      -- infixed function
      IF exists(right(node))
      THEN visit(right(node))
      FI
      -- postfixed function
END visit;
```
Program 2.
Binary tree traversal

Their construction from nodes and successors is similar. As for the case of trees, we consider only binary graphs, which means that a node will have at most two successors. The difference from trees is that two nodes may have a common successor, and a node may even be its own successor. There can thus be loops, and a node may be accessible by more than one path. Readers who wish to study the subject may consult Berge (1962).

The program which traverses all the nodes of a graph must avoid looping. In general, this is done by marking the nodes as they are visited. Each node requires a mark bit, which takes the value 1 the first time it is visited. When the program finds a marked node, it does not take it into account a second time, and does not visit the successors of a marked node, since they have already been visited. Program 3 gives the procedure for the traversal of a binary graph.

```
PROCEDURE visit(node);
    IF mark(node)=0
    THEN mark(node):=1;
            IF exists(lfoll(node))
            THEN visit(lfoll(node))
            FI;
            IF exists(rfoll(node))
            THEN visit(rfoll(node))
            FI
    FI
END visit;
```

Program 3.
Graph traversal

In this procedure, lfoll and rfoll are the left and right successors of a node, respectively. The procedure requires a starting point like the root of a tree. It uses the same conventions as those used for trees.

Marking a graph is in itself a useful process. For example, in programs written in languages such as LISP, memory is allocated as it is required. Objects take the form of graphs. During program execution, complete zones of memory can become inaccessible, that is no longer pointed to by addressable objects. Marking is the first stage of the process of garbage collection, which recovers space which is no longer used by the running program. All accessible objects are marked, starting with the root of a tree, or with the equivalent distinguished node of a graph. In a second pass, unmarked nodes are recovered (they are inaccessible), and marks are removed. The general algorithm given above has received a certain amount of attention (Griffiths 1979, Schorr and Waite 1967).

Matrix representation of graphs

In previous paragraphs, trees and graphs were represented by systems of pointers, sometimes stored in tables. Another possibility, particularly adapted to graphs with more than two successors per node, is their representation on a square, binary matrix. The matrix has one row and one column per graph node. Entry (i, j) is 1 if and only if the node j is a direct follower of the node i (there exists a branch from i to j), otherwise it is 0.

Consider the graph given in Figure 5.

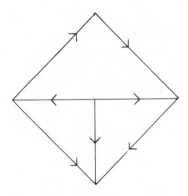

Figure 5.
A simple graph

Its representation on a binary matrix is shown in Figure 6.

As an example of the use of such matrices, consider the classic problem of transitive closure. This discovers all the nodes which can be reached by following branches from each given node. The direct followers are those given in Figure 6. To discover the set of accessible nodes, apply the transitive binary relation 'follower of'. For example, since node 2 is a successor of node 1, and node 3 is a successor of

33

	1	2	3	4	5
1	0	1	0	0	1
2	0	0	1	0	0
3	0	0	0	0	1
4	1	0	1	0	1
5	0	0	0	0	0

Figure 6.
Direct binary matrix

node 2, then node 3 is also a successor of node 1. If node 2 had other followers, they would all be followers of node 1. This is reflected in the matrix by adding row 2 into row 1 by the operation OR. The process is repeated as many times as necessary to obtain all possible successors, giving the final matrix in Figure 7.

	1	2	3	4	5
1	0	1	1	0	1
2	0	0	1	0	1
3	0	0	0	0	1
4	1	1	1	0	1
5	0	0	0	0	0

Figure 7.
Transitive closure

There exists a set of standard algorithms on binary matrices. The best known algorithm for transitive closure is that of

Warshall (1962). Notice that the absence of ones on the principal diagonal means that the graph contains no loops, and is thus a lattice. A binary matrix can be used, for example, to represent the different possibilities of a labyrinth. The matrix would be explored in order to find a path to the exit.

Stacks

Among other simple data structures, stacks are much used in artificial intelligence, and elsewhere. Objects can be added only on to the top of a stack. Similarly, they can only be taken off from the top. The object on the top of the stack is thus the most recently arrived amongst those which are still on the stack. It is for this reason that the term 'last in, first out' is often used to describe them.

Stack implementation is trivial. It requires two procedures, one to put objects on the stack (push), and the other to take them off (pull). The procedures work on a vector whose elements are of the appropriate type for stack objects. Program 4 gives the procedures for an integer stack.

```
PROCEDURE push(x:integer);
    stack(free):=x; free:=free+1
ENDPROC push;
PROCEDURE pull(x:integer);
    free:=free-1; x:=stack(free)
ENDPROC pull;
```

Program 4.
Stacks

The stack is declared as a vector of integers, free being the index of the first unoccupied space in the stack. To avoid pushing objects on to a full stack, or pulling them off an empty one, tests are required, which lead to Program 5.

Stacks are used to store information which is to be recovered in the order indicated (last in, first out). They will figure notably in backtracking algorithms. Note that, in general, stacks are used to implement programs which work on data which are completely bracketed. In ADA the above group of declarations would constitute a module.

```
stack: ARRAY (1..n) OF integer;
free: integer:=1;
PROCEDURE push(x:integer);
     IF free>n
     THEN error
     ELSE stack(free):=x; free:=free+1
     FI
ENDPROC push;
PROCEDURE pull(x:integer);
     IF free>1
     THEN free:=free-1; x:=stack(free)
     ELSE error
     FI
ENDPROC pull;
```

Program 5.
Stacks with tests

Recursion

To solve algorithmic problems needing complex logic, the most important tool is induction, or recurrence. Whereas simple recurrence can be easily translated into a loop, this is no longer true for situations often met in artificial intelligence. In particular, non-linear data structures such as trees and graphs lead to forms of recurrence which translate naturally into recursive programs. This problem was briefly mentioned on page 23. Readers with no experience of recursion may wish to consult textbooks such as Barron (1968). In some particular cases, it may be desirable to transform recursive programs into non-recursive ones. This is possible by the application of standard techniques, sometimes with difficulty. The subject is widely studied in the literature (Burstall and Darlington 1975, Griffiths 1976, Bauer and Broy 1979).

Of course, since all programs run on computers with linear memories, compilers can translate recursion into iteration, for which they use a stack. Similarly, programmers may choose to write their programs recursively or with an explicit stack. The two techniques are equivalent. The degree of efficiency which comes from the elimination of the stack, or of the recursion which leads to it, varies in different situations.

Exercises

1) Consider a peculiar set of binary genealogical trees in

which people have only one parent alive, and at most two children. Each node includes a field which contains the name of the person concerned. The root of the tree is called 'adam'. For such trees, write the following procedures:

a) Is there a node in the tree of name 'john'?

b) In the tree, is there a 'john' whose grandfather is called 'matthew'?

c) Do there exist first cousins called 'john' and 'jean'?

2) Consider a graph all of whose branches are bi-directional, that is that if there is a branch from node A to node B, then there is also a branch from B to A. The graph is represented by a binary matrix. Find out whether the graph is connex or not, that is whether all the nodes are mutually accessible, or if they constitute a set of independent (non-connected) graphs.

3) For a graph represented on a binary matrix, use transitive closure to carry out the marking algorithm given on page 32.

CHAPTER 3

General resolution methods

Non-determinist situations and backtracking
Certain resolution methods used in artificial intelligence problems were invented to overcome the difficulty of finding adequate determinist solutions. An algorithm is determinist if, at each step, it can correctly choose the relevant operation to execute, that is to identify the following step. Consider the example of a labyrinth. At any given moment, the direction which leads to the exit is unknown. One possible solution is to choose any direction, leaving a mark to say which (eg the pebbles of Hansel and Gretel). If such arbitrary choices come back to an already visited position, or if they lead to a cul de sac, then a different option must be tried, often after retracing the more recent steps, and so on recursively until the exit is found. This requires a series of trials, with correction in the case of error. The method is called trial and error, and the process of retracing steps, backtracking. Backtracking is a standard reply to a non-determinist situation, that is one in which it is not always possible to make the right decision first time.

Backtracking is only a first solution to this class of problems, since its direct use is inefficient in complex situations. Before going into such considerations, let us start with a program.

The mouse and the cheese
To illustrate backtracking, consider the following artificial labyrinth problem, which has the advantage of being small enough to be used for teaching. A mouse and a piece of cheese occupy arbitrary squares on a chessboard, with respective coordinates (xm,ym) and (xc,yc). The problem is to find a path which leads from the hungry mouse to the cheese, under certain constraints. The mouse moves one square at a time, either horizontally or vertically. In addition, certain moves are

impossible because barriers exist between the corresponding squares. The problem is an old one, first described in computing in Zemanek (1971).

The first program to solve this problem employs backtracking to find a path, without trying to find the shortest one. For expository reasons, the programming language resumed on page 25 is used. Note that specialized artificial intelligence languages, such as **PROLOG**, are capable of automatic backtracking. This has the advantage of making life easier for programmers, but hides the technique in a pedagogical situation.

The program has the following characteristics:

1) At each step it prefers to go forward, but when this is impossible, it backtracks.
2) A forward movement is always in the first available direction from the current square.
3) The order of availability is always north, east, south, west, represented by the integers 1,2,3,4, respectively.
4) On arrival in a square, the program marks it. Marks are never rubbed out. The mouse never returns to a marked square, since the algorithm tries all possibilities from each square visited, and care must be taken not to loop.
5) Backtracking consists of a return to the square from which it came, followed by a new effort in the next available direction from that square.
6) Backtracking takes place because none of the four possible directions from a square can lead to the cheese by a new path.
7) To take a backwards step, it is necessary to know which was the preceding square. The direction taken at each move is put on the stack. Each backtrack goes back on the most recent decision, which is on the top of the stack. If the situation is still blocked, the program goes back again, and so on.

The complete program is given in Program 6, comments being regrouped at the end in order to facilitate presentation. The row numbers identify comments.

1. barrier (i,j,dir) is true if and only if there is a barrier between square (i,j) and its neighbour in the direction dir. The program to initialize this array is not given. The edges

```
1 BEGIN barrier: ARRAY (1..8,1..8,1..4) OF bool;
2     mark: ARRAY (1..8,1..8) OF bool;
3     stack: ARRAY (1..64) OF integer;
4     x,y,xn,yn,xm,ym,xc,yc: integer;
5     dir: integer;
6     poss:bool;
7     read(xm,ym,xc,yc);
8     x:=xm; y:=ym; mark(x,y):=TRUE; dir:=0;
                                    poss:=TRUE;
9     WHILE NOT(x=xc AND y=yc) AND poss
10    DO IF dir<4
11      THEN dir:=dir+1;
12              xn:= CASE dir OF (x,x+1,x,x-1) ESAC;
13              yn:= CASE dir OF (y+1,y,y-1,y) ESAC;
14              IF NOT barrier(x,y,dir)
                                CAND NOT mark(xn,yn)
15              THEN x:=xn; y:=yn; mark(x,y):=TRUE;
16                   push(dir); dir:=0
                FI
17        ELSE poss:=NOT(x=xm AND y=ym);
18             IF poss
19             THEN pull(dir);
20                  CASE dir
21                  OF 1: y:=y-1,
22                     2: x:=x-1,
23                     3: y:=y+1,
24                     4: x:=x+1
                    ESAC;
                FI
          FI
      DONE;
25    IF poss
26    THEN -- path on stack
27    ELSE -- no path exists
      FI
  END
```

Program 6.
The mouse and the cheese

of the chessboard are protected by barriers, which avoids
testing separately that the considered square exists.
2. mark (i,j) is true if and only if the mouse has already

41

visited square (i,j). This array must be initialized to false.

3. The procedures push and pull are given on page 35. Push puts a value on the stack and pull takes one off. Since there are 64 squares, the stack has 64 elements.

4. (x,y) is the current position of the mouse, (xm,ym) its initial position and (xc,yc) the initial position of the cheese. (xn,yn) is a square to be considered by the mouse for its next step.

5. dir is the number of directions already tried from the current square.

6. poss is a Boolean which indicates whether it is still possible to look for a path. It will become false if all possibilities are tried and fail.

7. Read the initial positions of the mouse and the cheese.

8. Initialization puts the mouse at its start point, which is marked. No direction has been tried. All possibilities are not yet exhausted.

9. Loop as long as the cheese is not found and all possibilities are not exhausted.

10. Is there a new direction to try?

11. Take the next one.

12, 13. dir=1 is north, that is increase y by one, and so on.

14. Test absence of barrier in the chosen direction. If there is none, test afterwards (CAND) if square (xn,yn) is marked. If the barrier indicated the edge of the chessboard, (xn,yn) would not exist. CAND avoids referring to such non-existent squares.

15. If the movement is possible, it is carried out, marking the new square. Otherwise going round the loop will take the next direction.

16. Stack the decision. For the new square, the number of already tried directions is zero.

17. Since there are no more directions to try, backtracking is necessary. This is possible unless the algorithm is already back to the start position.

18. If possible.

19. Pull the direction taken to get to the current square.

20-24. Reverse lines 10 and 11 to deduce the predecessor of the current square and go back for a new loop.

25. poss=TRUE means a path has been found.

26. It is described on the stack.

27. Otherwise, no path exists.

At the end of the program, if a path exists, the stack contains all the correct decisions made, that is those which have not been eliminated by backtracking. The stack contains a solution to the problem. The loop required to print the solution is not programmed, but the principle that the stack contains all valid decisions is correct in all backtracking algorithms. During the execution of the program, the stack contains all those decisions which are under consideration.

Research space
Consider again the above labyrinth problem. From each square, there are at most four directions from which to leave it. From the new square there are again at most four possibilities, and so on. These possibilities can be described using a decision tree, as shown in Figure 8, in which the first two levels are shown.

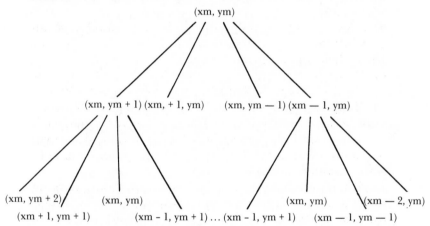

Figure 8.
Two levels of the labyrinth decision tree

In Figure 8, four branches are given from each node, but in practice several branches should not be there, for the following reasons:

1) A barrier, or the edge of the chessboard, may eliminate the possibility.
2) Loops must be avoided. This means eliminating any node which is its own ancestor. In particular, going back to the direct predecessor is not allowed. This means that

the only node which can have four possible successors is the initial square occupied by the mouse. The tree is thus finite, but a square may occur more than once, on different paths. A path goes from the root to a leaf. This condition is weaker than that of the program, since the marking done by the program is dynamic, and does not consider a sub-tree whose root node has already been visited.

The backtracking algorithm explores the tree by taking the left-most branch each time. When it is blocked, it goes up a level in the tree to try the next branch, and so on recursively. This tree traversal is called 'depth first search'. A path from the mouse to the cheese is a path through the tree from father to son, starting at the root (xm,ym) and finishing at the cheese (xc,yc). In the complete tree, there are all the non-looping paths which have their origin at (xm,ym).

Since the program traverses the tree in a predefined order, it will always find the left-most solution. What is more, the marking algorithm assures us that, if the same square occurs on more than one path, the underlying sub-tree is only examined once. This depends on the fact that, before back-tracking from a given node, the complete dependent sub-tree has been explored. Thus, backtracking from a square means that there is no path from that square to the cheese without going back to a predecessor. This discussion confirms the correctness of the marking algorithm in the program.

In the simple case of the example labyrinth, it is possible to explore all the existing paths, or to print the complete derivation tree for the research space. In practical problems in the real world, the research space is much larger, and may not be finite. This means that complete trees are not available, and that complete exploration is outside the capacities of available computers. On page 55 we consider an example of this combinatorial explosion. While backtracking remains a fundamental technique for solving non-determinist problems, it is not in itself sufficient in many cases.

As an example of combinatorial complexity, consider the game of chess. The possible number of games is infinite, since loops are possible, but the number of different positions is finite. The order of magnitude of the number of different positions is around 10 to the 100. Another calculation which has been made is that the number of games without loops (repetition of positions) is bigger than the number of atoms in the universe. This eliminates all algorithms which wish to play chess by the complete evaluation of the derivation tree. Apart from simple endgame positions, no chess situation can be completely evaluated by a computer in an acceptable time limit. Means of reducing traversals are required which will allow the evaluation of useful branches and ignore the others.

Heuristics and evaluation

In the absence of complete evaluation, the best choice of a chess move is, in general, not proven. The discovery of a determinist algorithm by a research worker in the future seems improbable, and we have just seen that complete evaluation of the tree is outside the capacity of computers, now and in the foreseeable future. This means that the computer will not play perfect chess, that is determinist chess, as far as we can see.

In order to reduce combinatorial complexity, heuristics are often useful. These take the form of incomplete rules which tend to indicate the right choice, but without giving a guarantee. Colloquially, we may talk of rules of thumb. For chess, this means applying general principles concerning, for example, material value (eg a queen is worth two rooks or three minor pieces) or positional considerations (eg control of the centre, linked pawns). These rules come from analyses by expert players, and lead to an acceptable level of performance.

From this brief discussion of heuristics, it results that artificial intelligence programs must frequently take decisions on incomplete information. They follow approximate rules of evaluation. Carrying on with the example of chess, a decision consists of the choice of a move, which operates a transition from one position to another. The choice is between the set of possible new positions. This mechanism requires an evaluation of the positions in function of different criteria. It is position evaluation which is one of the most difficult problems in writing programs of this type.

Levy (1983) gives examples of evaluation formulae for different games. In simple cases, the formula may be the distance which separates the current position from the final one. For example, looking for a minimal path from the mouse to the cheese may be done by a heuristic such as to take as first choice a move which goes towards the cheese. The evaluation function in this case is the distance which separates the current position of the mouse from the cheese. For chess, the function takes into account multiple criteria which each has a numerical value. The result is a figure which represents approximately the value of the position.

Minimax

In a game with two players, taking into account position evaluation can be done by the minimax algorithm. Suppose that the decision tree is to be examined to a depth of four moves, that is two moves per player (Figure 9). Some authors speak of half moves, which means that in their texts one move is the same as two moves here. In the given position, white is to play.

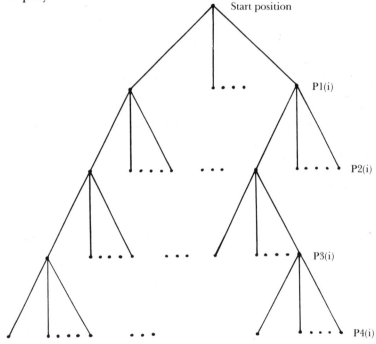

Figure 9.
Decision tree of depth four

In Figure 9, the P1(i) are the different positions which result from white's possible first moves, the P2(i) from black's first moves, and so on. The positions obtained after black's possible second moves (ie the leaves of the depth four tree) are evaluated. All marks are given from white's point of view, that is that a large score is good for white and bad for black. Level three scores, that is the next level up, are deduced by taking the minimum values of the corresponding sub-trees. This is because black is assumed to play to his best interests, that is to minimize white's score. For example, consider the sub-tree P3(i) which takes its value from the P4(i) below, as in Figure 10.

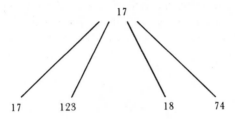

Figure 10.
Minimum of a sub-tree

The P4 positions resulted from a black move. As he is assumed to have played his best move, the minimum score, 17 in this example, is passed upwards to the P3 concerned. To deduce the level 2 score, the level three scores of the sub-trees are similarly taken into account, except that this time it is white to play. Since he also plays in his best interests, the score passed upwards will be the maximum available. Scores are thus regrouped at each level, before being passed to the next level above. The score transmitted is alternatively the minimum and then the maximum of those available. This calculation indicates the move which is the best as far as it is possible to judge from the available information.

This method forms the basis of numerous programs, but applied directly is only of limited efficiency because the number of tree nodes is often large. Means are required to avoid the evaluation of all the branches. In the jargon of artificial intelligence, this is called pruning the decision tree. The next section proposes improvements of this type.

Pruning
Evaluating all the branches of the tree to a given depth is a waste of time for at least two reasons: some sub-trees are of

47

insufficient value and others can be eliminated by heuristics. Consider first a general algorithm which eliminates completely certain branches, the alpha-beta cutoff.

In the above decision tree for chess, Figure 11 gives the level 2 sub-tree which contains that of level 3 in Figure 10.

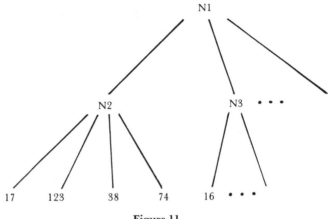

Figure 11.
Level 2 sub-tree

The left-most level 3 sub-tree transmits to N2 the value 17. But, next on the right, the occurrence of 16 means that N3 will always receive a value less than the 17 of N2. N3 can be eliminated immediately, together with the whole of its sub-tree, from the rest of the calculation. It is this elimination which is called alpha-beta cutoff.

The improvement obtained by the application of this algorithm is larger than it may seem, since it grows rapidly with the size of the tree. Since chess trees are particularly full, the improvement can be a factor of a hundred when compared with simple minimax. The number of positions at depth four in a typical game of chess is about a million, most of which are of little interest. The effect of the algorithm is, of course, reinforced by its recursive application at successive levels.

Up to now, trees have been explored systematically and in a fixed order. This is not necessarily the best choice. In particular, the described program evaluates all the positions at the leaves of the tree. It is, in fact, more efficient to evaluate positions as they are produced, higher up in the tree. Levels n+1, n+2 ... will only be considered if the mark at level n is *a priori* favourable. This technique may miss the best move in certain sacrifice situations, but allows exploration of the tree to different depths depending on the interest of the sub-tree considered. As always, the introduction of heuristic methods for efficiency reasons may reduce the level of security. But in chess, since the number of moves considered in advance is relatively small, a good heuristic choice which allows certain sub-trees to be explored further leads to a program which is both more efficient and a better chess player. Note that, with evaluation at each level, it is better to explore the most favourable positions first, which means ordering decision tree traversal. This will lead to a maximum number of branches cut off by the alpha-beta mechanism.

A symbolic example

Consider the following logical problem from a popular magazine (J & S 1984a). Four married couples meet for an evening. At a given moment, the eight people are involved in four distinct conversations, under the following conditions:

1) Beatrice is talking with Eric;
2) Ann with Charlotte's husband;
3) Frank with George's wife;
4) Danielle with Ann's husband;
5) and George with Eric's wife.

The problem is to find out who is talking to Humphrey. Rule numbers are used below.

HUMAN SOLUTION
Having understood that to answer the question required the resolution of the system, that is who is married to whom and who is in conversation with whom, the authors started by enumerating possibilities. Since Ann, Danielle and Beatrice are all conversing with men, the same must be true for Charlotte, since there is no spare woman. Each conversation is thus between a man and a woman. The table of all marriage possibilities is given in Figure 12. It will enable us to deduce the conversations. Names of participants are represented by their first letter, the author of the question having kindly chosen women A,B,C,D and men E,F,G,H.

49

	1	2	3	4	5	6	7	8	9	10	11	12	13	14	15	16	17	18	19	20	21	22	23	24
A	E	E	E	E	E	E	F	F	F	F	F	F	G	G	G	G	G	G	H	H	H	H	H	H
B	F	F	G	G	H	H	E	E	G	G	H	H	E	E	F	F	H	H	E	E	F	F	G	G
C	G	H	F	H	F	G	G	H	E	H	E	G	F	H	E	H	E	F	F	G	E	G	E	F
D	H	G	H	F	G	F	H	G	H	E	G	E	H	F	H	E	F	E	G	F	G	E	F	E

Figure 12.
The 24 marriage possibilities

There are factorial (4), that is 24, possible combinations. For each case, consider the implications of the constraints of the question (rules 1 to 5 above), which were about conversations. The implications require the replacement of x's husband or y's wife by the names of the relevant partners.

In the following, the woman's name will always be on the left. For case 1, rules 1 to 5 become the following:

B talks to E
A to G
C to F
D to E
A to G

Since Eric talks on the one hand with Beatrice, and on the other hand, as Ann's husband, with Danielle, this case can be eliminated. Note that if Eric is Ann's husband, there can never be a solution, since rules 1 and 4 contradict each other. This remark eliminates the first six cases.

It is not difficult to realize that this elimination technique can be generalized to eliminate cases by blocks rather than treating them independently. After a number of trials which depend on the experience and the problem solving capacities of the individual, he will draw up a table of elimination theorems:

T1. E is not C's husband (rules 1+2)
T2. B is not G's wife (1+3)
T3. E is not A's husband (1+4)
T4. B is not E's wife (+5)

These theorems come from the implications of combinations of the original rules, as in the example of case 1, where it was deduced that Ann and Eric cannot be married. Figure 13 shows which cases can be eliminated by these theorems, some of them being eliminated more than once.

Case	1	2	3	4	5	6	7	8	9	10	11	12	13	14	15
Elimination by theorem	3	3	2,3	2,3	3	3	4	4	1,2	2	1		4	4	1

Case	16	17	18	19	20	21	22	23	24
Elimination by theorem	1		4	4	1			1,2	2

Figure 13.
Elimination by theorems

The cases not yet eliminated are 12, 16, 18 and 22. Figure 14 gives the constraints for these cases.

	Case	12	16	18	22
	A	F	G	G	H
Marriages	B	H	F	H	F
	C	G	H	F	G
	D	E	E	E	E
	A	G	H,F	F,F	G
Conversations	B	E	E	E	E
	C	F			F
	D	F,G	G,G	G,G	H,G

Figure 14.
Last cases

As can be seen, in case 12 George is talking with Ann and Danielle, Frank with Charlotte and Danielle, and Danielle with Frank and George. The case is eliminated three times. In the same way, cases 16 and 22 disappear, leaving case 18 as the solution. Thus, the reply to the question is that Humphrey is talking to Charlotte.

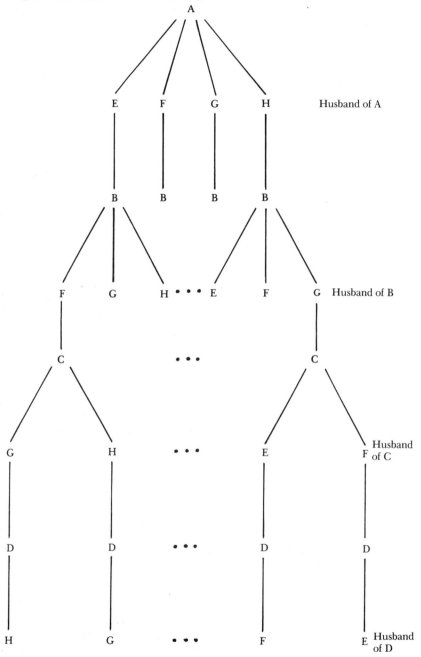

Figure 15.
Possibility tree

ANALYSIS

The above solution was derived from a mixture of two techniques: case enumeration with elimination of cases by the application of conditions and theorem proving to shorten the calculation. Mixed methods of this type are often encountered in human demonstrations, but are more difficult to implement on a computer.

The enumeration of Figure 12 is a new form of the decision tree described previously. Figure 15 shows it in the usual tree form.

The 24 possible paths from the root to a leaf represent the 24 possible marriage combinations. As for the problem of the mouse and the cheese, examining the 24 possibilities one after the other comes down to backtracking over the tree by depth first search.

A programmed solution to the problem could thus be a complete tree traversal, examining constraints on each path in order to find incoherencies. This approach does not use the short cuts which come from the additional logic used by the human solver to avoid painful repetition. These short cuts are in fact representative of a separate technique, which is theorem proving.

A human solver mixes up the two methods during problem resolution, but a program will usually only use one at a time. A parallel with general programming could be that enumeration is a bottom-up method, and theorem proving top-down. The problem is solved by pure theorem proving in the next section.

SOLUTION BY THEOREM PROVING

The conditions are written with the following operators:

t: X t Y means X is talking to Y
m: X m Y means X is married to Y
$p\!r$: X $p\!r$ Y means X is not married to Y

The system of constraints becomes:

R1: B t E
R2: A t H(C)   H(C) = husband of C
R3: W (G) t F   W(G) = wife of G
R4: D t H(A)

R5:   W (E) t G
R6:   X t H

From these rules, deductions can be drawn. A first job could be to establish who is the wife of E, as follows:

C m E   (R1+R2)
A m E   (R1+R4)
B m E   (R1+R5)

Since E has a right to be married, it can only be to D. Thus:

D1: D m E
D2: D t G   (D1+R5)
D3: A m G   (D2+R4)
D4: A t F   (D3+R3)

The solution is thus C t H (R1+D2+D4), with the following marriages:

C m F   (D4+R2)
B m H   (left over)

Formally, the solution is not proven, since it was assumed that a solution exists. A complete proof would carry out the process of confirming that the deduced marriages and conversations are compatible with rules R1 to R6. The proof is trivial.

This deduction method gives a compact solution. However, in order to find it, many more formulae are manipulated than those needed for the solution. Before producing the above deductions in the given order, we spent some time on different deduction lines, and are still not sure that the result is minimal. The problem is to choose between useful deductions and non-productive ones.

A program based on these principles would enumerate those theorems which can be deduced from the set of supplied axioms, which are the constraints of the system. To do this, it will try all the different combinations of known facts, deducing new ones, which are then added to the stock. The new facts are used to deduce others, and so on. The process leads, in general, to large numbers of theorems, and often to a possibly infinite number. To be efficient, a theorem prover needs means of choosing those theorems which are likely to be useful in the context of the considered hypothesis.

Combinatorial explosion
In the specialized press, much has been made of combinatorial explosion in artificial intelligence programs, that is to say the exponential increase in the number of cases to examine when going down levels in the decision tree. The controversy even led to doubts as to the possibility of applying artificial intelligence in real-life situations because of combinatorial complexity. The problem is illustrated here by another simple game, solitaire.

SOLITAIRE
As its name indicates, solitaire is a game with one player. It is played on a board the shape of a St George's cross. Figure 16 shows a possible starting position.

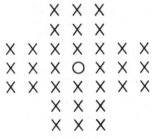

Figure 16.
A starting position for solitaire

Crosses represent pawns, and the o an empty space. At the beginning of a game, all the positions except one are occupied by identical pawns. The empty space can be in any position, but the centre of the board is the most usual. A move is carried out by a pawn jumping over a horizontal or vertical neighbour into an empty space. The jumped over pawn is removed from play. The aim of the game is to reach a final position which is the inverse of the start position, that is with exactly one pawn left, in the place of the initial space.

The game is not difficult, human players managing to find a solution after a certain number of tries. No particular problem solving capacity is necessary. The next section introduces a programmed solution which uses backtracking.

PROGRAM
The program should be immediately comprehensible to the reader who has followed the problem of the mouse and the cheese. The text is given in Program 7 for those who wish to get practice, but that is not the main purpose of this section.

```
BEGIN t: ARRAY (0..33) OF integer;
     -- t(i) is 1 if there is a pawn in the corresponding
     -- position, and 0 if not. t(0) represents all inexistant
     -- positions, and contains -1. The initialisation of t is
     -- not programmed here.
     neighbour,sn: ARRAY (1..33, 1..4) OF integer;
     -- To avoid painful calculation, the squares are numbered
     -- from 1 to 33. The arrays neighbour and sn indicate the
     -- number of the position and surposition (position after a
     -- jump) for each position in each direction. If the
     -- neighbour or sn do not exist (are over the edge of the
     -- board), the array entry contains -1. The arrays must be
     -- initialised by a program which is not provided here.
     done: bool; i,dir: integer;
     done:=FALSE; i:=1; dir:=0;
     -- done will be true at the end of the process, i is the
     -- index of the considered position, dir the number of
     -- directions already tried to find a move for the pawn on
     -- square i.
     WHILE NOT done
     DO IF dir<4
     -- There are still directions to try from the current
     -- position.
        THEN dir:=dir+1;
            IF t(i)=1 AND t(neighbour(i,dir))=1 AND t(sn(i,dir))=0
     -- A jump is possible.
            THEN t(i):=0; t(neighbour(i,dir)):=0;
                t(sn(i,dir)):=1; push(i,dir);
     -- Stack the decision.
                i:=1; dir:=0; done:= t=endpos
     -- Preparation for finding a new jump, from the beginning.
     -- endpos is the position aimed at.
            FI
        ELSE IF i=33
     -- Backtrack.
            THEN pull(i,dir); t(i):=1;
                t(neighbour(i,dir)):=1; t(sn(i,dir)):=0
     -- Go back on the most recent decision.
            ELSE dir:=0; i:=i+1
     -- Try the next position.
            FI
        FI
     DONE
END
```

Program 7.
Solitaire

EVALUATION

As each move takes off one pawn, and the starting position has 32 pawns on the board, the solution needs 31 moves. If there are 5 different possibilities for each move (approximate), the number of different games is about 5**31. The following approximate calculation estimates the time necessary to play them:

```
5**31 = (10/2)**31
      = (10**31)/(2**31)
      = (10**31)/(10**9) approximately
      = 10**22
```

If it needs 1000 machine instructions per move, and the computer carries out 1,000,000 instructions a second, the calculation time is as follows:

```
(10**22)/1000 seconds = 10**19 seconds
                      = (10**19)/3600 hours
                      = 3*(10**15) hours approximately
                      = 3*(10**15)/(24*365) years
                      = (10**12)/3 years approximately
```

that is, 300,000,000,000 years to go through all the possible solutions.

Of course, the first solution found is sufficient, rejected solutions are of less than 31 moves, computers execute more than 1000,000 instructions a second and the algorithm can be improved. However, even after taking all this into account, the time necessary is still quite impossible. It is calculations of this type that lead to the belief that combinatorial complexity could prohibit the practical exploitation of artificial intelligence.

This is not our point of view, but it would be naive and unrealistic to ignore the problem. Two conclusions are immediately obvious:

1) Approximate calculations of the type carried out above ought to be done for each new algorithm, in order to decide whether its use is reasonable or not.
2) An important part of the computer expert's job lies in the search for more efficient solutions. Many of the problems

which are considered have first solutions which are theoretically ideal, but cannot be implemented with acceptable performance.

The example considered here is a classic teaching trick. It is often given to students as a programming exercise. More than once a student has run the program on a personal computer in anticipation of following lecture, without first having carried out the calculation. The lesson is usually never forgotten.

Compared to the usual problems of efficiency dealt with by computer scientists, combinatorial explosion is an extreme phenomenon. It cannot be controlled by the use of optimizing compilers, or by the transformation of programs to get rid of recursion. Of course, even in classical programming, the most important improvements in efficiency are to be found at the algorithmic level, and not, as some programmers still believe, by writing machine code. Technical improvements gain percentages, whereas algorithmic improvements gain factors. Artificial intelligence problems require thinking at the level of the basic methods of resolution, before even getting down to algorithmics.

Learning

Learning is the way in which machines or people take account of experience. It can be considered to be the artificial intelligence equivalent of feedback in control systems. Learning programs need to remember decisions made during previous efforts at problem solving, and to take into account the degree of satisfaction obtained in the past when applying them again. As before, the subject is introduced by an example.

TIC-TAC-TOE BY LEARNING

Consider the game of noughts and crosses (TIC-TAC-TOE), for which the program of Michie (1962) was quoted in Chapter 1. Its solution by program is simple, but instructive. For the readers who never played the game during their schooldays, the rules are as follows: two players put alternatively their mark, one playing O and the other X, in a free square of a 3*3 matrix. The aim is to make a horizontal, vertical or diagonal line of 3. The theoretical result of the game is a draw, the first player having more chances of profiting from an opponent's error.

An obvious approach to the problem would be to evaluate, for each move, the whole decision tree, using a minimax algorithm. This gives a theoretically perfect program. The program is not given here, but interested readers may wish to write it as an exercise. The program which follows is a solution by learning which remembers systematically all experiments, without using any heuristics or other intelligent aids.

The program keeps a list of all possible positions with, for each of them, a list of possible moves. These lead to known new positions. With each move is associated a score, which evolves in function of the results of games in which it was played. The system starts with all scores at zero. At the end of a game, if the program wins, the scores of the moves played are increased by one. If it loses, they are reduced by one. In any given position, the program plays the move which has the highest score, choosing randomly between equals.

The program plays a certain number of games against human opponents, improving its knowledge of the game by the resulting scores. In practice, Michie found that his program 'learnt' how to play a perfect game after 200 experiences. Of course, the number of games necessary depends on the way in which its opponents play, as well as on the program's knowledge of symmetry.

PROGRAM

Program 8 is a concrete solution of noughts and crosses by learning. It uses preliminary work which is not programmed here. The result of the program is to store in secondary memory two files, which are read into main memmory before each game. The first is an array of all the possible positions. For each position, there is an entry per square on the board. This entry contains the index of the position which results from playing in the corresponding square, or –1 if the square is already filled. The second file contains the scores which correspond to each possible move in each position. The two files are of the same size.

Since there are 9 squares, and 3 possibilities per square (O, X or free), a preliminary calculation indicates that the number of possible positions is $3**9$, which is 19,683. In fact the number of positions which can exist is notably less, since playing alternatively means that the numbers of O and of X are balanced. Also, positions containing a full line are eliminated, together with full positions. The real figure is around 6000 positions, without considering symmetry.

The program uses the array of positions (pos) described above. Its preparation is done by another program, not given here. The program reads the current state of the array of marks, with pos, from the disk. Each mark was zero before learning started, and the new state of the array is returned to the disk after each game.

```
BEGIN -- play a new game
     loss, win: bool;
     i,j,r: integer;
     np: integer CONSTANT= -- array size
     nbpawns: integer; -- the number of pawns played
     pos, mark: ARRAY (0..np, 1..9) OF integer;
     -- pos(0) is the empty board
     save: ARRAY (1..2, 1..9) OF integer;
     PROCEDURE keep(position, move: integer);
          save(1,nbpawns):=position; save(2,nbpawns):=move
     ENDPROC keep;
     read_disk(pos,mark); nbpawns:=0;
     IF opponent's move
     THEN display(empty_board);
          read(r); nbpawns:=1;       -- accept the first move
          i:=r        -- resulting position
     ELSE i:=0
     FI;
     stop:=FALSE;
     WHILE NOT stop
     DO j:=max(i);          -- find the highest mark
        nbpawns:=nbpawns+1; keep(i,j);
        win:=line(j,me); -- test for a win, me being the program
        stop:= win OR nbpawns=9;
        IF NOT stop
        THEN error:=TRUE;
             WHILE error
             DO display(j); read(r);        -- get next move
                erreur:=pos(j,r)=-1      -- illegal move
             DONE;
             nbpawns:=nbpawns+1;
             loss:=line(r,-me);        -- test for a loss
                                       -- -me is the opponent
             stop:=loss OR nbpawns=9;
             i:=pos(j,r)          -- next position
        FI
     DONE;
     IF loss
     THEN FOR i:= (IF even(nbpawns)
                     THEN 1          -- the program started
                     ELSE 2
                     FI) BY 2 TO nbpawns-1
          DO    -- reduce marks of played moves
     mark(save(1,i),save(2,i)):=mark(save(1,i),save(2,i))-1
          DONE
```

```
    ELSE IF win
        THEN FOR i:= (IF even(nbpawns)
                         THEN 2
                         ELSE 1
                         FI) BY 2 TO nbpawns
              DO   -- increase marks
    mark(save(1,i),save(2,i)):=mark(save(1,i),save(2,i))+1
              DONE
          FI
    FI;
    write_disk(mark)
END
```

Program 8.
TIC-TAC-TOE

GENERALIZATION

From this example can be deduced the characteristics of a learning program. There are three important aspects:

1) Being able to store situations in which decisions need to be made.
2) Being able to evaluate the results of these decisions.
3) Being able to store the results in order to apply them usefully when the situation comes round again.

As with heuristic methods, learning may be used to improve existing algorithms and methods. In practical applications, learning is used to refine the values of parameters, or to increase the performance of algorithms by discovering which are the branches which are more often successful than others.

Exercises
1) Redo the mouse and cheese program incorporating the heuristic which consists of making the first trial in the direction of the cheese.
2) Write the mouse and cheese program with a recursive procedure instead of an explicit stack.
3) Compare the performances of the recursive and iterative versions of the mouse and the cheese problem.
4) Write a determinist program which finds a shortest path from the mouse to the cheese.
5) Some readers will have realized that it is more sensible to enumerate conversations in the couples problem, in particular since we already know that B talks to E. Redo the enumeration solution starting with conversations.

61

6) Find a solution to the game of solitaire which reduces it to a reasonable computer time.
7) Program noughts and crosses by minimax.
8) Compare the performances of the two noughts and crosses programs.
9) There are many games which can be solved by backtracking, in particular on chessboards. Consider the problem of putting 8 queens on a chessboard such that no two are on the same row, the same column or the same diagonal.

CHAPTER 4

Theorem proving

Solving complex problems by theorem proving, or by symbol manipulation, employs methods derived as much from mathematics as from computing. This chapter gives some basic methods, which are completed by reference to more specialist works for readers who require a deeper knowledge of the subject. An expert system user, such as an expert system creator, does not need to write theorem proving programs. However, some knowledge of how they work can improve his ability to write rules and/or questions.

First order logic
Obviously, an automatic theorem proving system needs some formal base. Whereas the first provers were applied to a limited number of theorems, in the hands of specialists, expert systems call the theorem prover frequently, on questions put by non-expert users. Therefore, modern provers need to be much more efficient than their predecessors. They must also allow problem description in terms accessible to these users. This problem recurs in Chapter 5.

Automatic theorem proving follows research on logic and the validity of proofs, which is particularly ancient. At the end of the seventeenth century, Leibniz was already looking for an algorithm to prove or refute formulae. The modern era dates from Herbrand (1930), who gives an algorithm of this kind for formulae in first order logic. It is this logic, called predicate calculus if it contains no additional specific axioms, that is the basis of todays's theorem provers.

First order logic has several advantages. First, it is the basis of all mathematical logic. Thus, it corresponds to intuition developed through experience over a long period of time. What is more, this tradition means that it has been widely studied. There is an impressive body of theorems and methods available. Finally, first order logic is built on a well known axiomatic system which allows reliable and efficient use.

Formjal presentations of first order logic are numerous. The one given here follows Loveland (1978). The basic elements are as follows:

1) variables written x,y,z;
2) constants written a,b,c;
3) functions written f,g,h;
4) predicates written P,Q,R,E;
5) the propositional calculus connectors, NOT, &, OR;
6) quantifiers THEREEXISTS, V .

The predicate E stands for the equality of its two parameters.

Basic elements are used to create terms, defined recursively as follows:

1) Variables and functions are terms.
2) If t1, t2 ... tn are terms, then f (t1, t2 ... tn) is a term.

Using terms, formulae can be written. They have the following recursive definition:

1) A predicate P without a parameter is a formula.
2) If t1, t2 ... tn are terms, then the predicate Q(t1, t2 ... tn) is a formula.
3) If A and B are formulae, then so are (NOT A), (A & B), (A OR B).
4) If A is a formula, then so are V x(A) and THEREEXISTS x(A).

The definitions of basic objects allow the construction of formulae which will be true or false with respect to the values of their constituent terms and the given calculations. The first order theory presented in this chapter has no additional axioms, that is no axioms which describe any particular field. Thus, we can use the term predicate calculus in the presentation.

In order to avoid excessive use of brackets, the connectors have a conventional order of priorities. These are as follows, starting with the strongest:

NOT THEREEXISTS V
OR
&
=> ≡

For this syntax, there exists an algorithm which decides if a formula is well formed.

Once the syntax rules for writing formulae are established, rules of manipulation can be proposed. These serve as axioms to allow the coherent transformation of formulae. These transformations are preliminary steps which need to be carried out in preparation for a demonstration. Theoretical work in the field provides rules which control the validity and the consistence of axiom sets. For example, they ought to be finite, and transformations of well-formed formulae must produce well-formed formulae.

A first axiom set is the common patrimony of propositional and predicate calculus. It is, in fact, a subset of predicate calculus which treats statements globally, without analysis. It allows truth or falsehood deduction from component values and the rules about NOT, OR, &, => and ≡. Its variables are thus propositional, whereas those of predicate calculus are individual and can be universally or existentially quantified. Predicate calculus allows the analysis of the internal structure of propositions which were left undivided by propositional calculus.

Among the axioms of propositional calculus are the conversions rules between the operators NOT, OR, &, ≡, =>. For example, the two latter operators are not in the original set, but are defined in terms of others, as follows:

A => B = (NOT A OR B)
A ≡ B = (NOT A OR B) & (NOT B OR A)

The other axioms are those of the double negative (1), the application of NOT over the connectors & and OR, that is the laws of de Morgan (2, 3), together with the distributivity of & over OR (4) and its inverse (5):

1) NOT NOT A = A
2) NOT (A OR B) = NOT A & NOT B
3) NOT (A & B) = NOT A OR NOT B

65

4) A & (B OR C) = (A & B) OR (A & C)
5) A OR (B & C) = (A OR B) & (A OR C)

Another category of axioms is the description of different application fields, for example group theory, set theory, plane geometry. Mathematicians have considerable experience in the definition of axiom sets of this kind.

Everybody is used to the logical connectors & and OR, but some readers may not be familiar with the use of the quantifiers THEREEXISTS AND V. Consider, in the first instance, the role of variables in formulae with quantifiers, as in the following example, where A is a formula:

THEREEXISTS x(A)

This reads 'there exists at least on x such that A is true'. In general A will contain a reference to x, since otherwise the quantifier is of no use. x is said to be sound by the quantifier wthin A. A variable which is not bound is said to be free. Consider the following example:

THEREEXISTS x P(x,y) & Q(x)

The scope of THEREEXISTS is the proposition P (see the table of priorities). Thus, the first two occurrences of x are bound, the third, after Q, being free. A formula which contains no free variables is said to be closed.

Of course, it is not the syntax of formulae and of manipulation rules which are of interest to users, but the way in which they are to be understood, that is the semantics. Amongst the semantic rules of propositional calculus are the results of evaluating the operators NOT, & and OR. They contain the rule that the NOT of a true proposition is false, and vice versa, that the & of two propositions is true if and only if the two are true, and so on. However, syntax is essential for two reasons. Firstly, since the aim is that of automatic theorem proving, strict syntax is required to allow computer treatment. Second, this syntactic basis allows mathematicians to give conditions for obtaining proofs, that is interpretations.

Thus, there exists a way of writing formulae and sets of manipulation rules (for a given field). A proof is the confirmation or the refutation of a formula, proposed as a hypothesis. In the couples problem from page 49 the axioms are the descriptions of marriages and conversations. A possible hypothesis would be:

Ann is talking to Humphrey.

The interpretation consists of the evaluation of the formula, which leads to one of the values TRUE or FALSE (in fact, FALSE). The hypothesis is thus refuted.

To prove such a refutation, the system needs inference rules which allow it to deduce, from the given premisses (facts, axioms and the hypothesis), a conclusion which follows logically from these premisses. The most simple inference rule is *modus ponens*, or splitting, which considers.

NOT P OR Q together with P

and deduces (or splits off) Q.

As an example, consider the statements:

'if it is fine, then the sun shines'.
'It is fine'.

Replacing the implication by an OR leads to:

NOT ('it is fine') OR ('the sun shines')
'it is fine'

with the deduction 'the sun shines'.

Modus ponens can be explained in terms of the semantics of implication. Thus, if P implies Q, and P is true, then Q is also true. There exist varieties of *modus ponens* such as the syllogism, that is that:

$$P \text{ OR } Q$$

and $\quad$ NOT Q OR R

leads to $\quad$ P OR R

Translating this to implications gives:

$$\text{NOT } P => Q$$

and $\quad$ Q => R

leads to $\quad$ NOT P => R

67

which confirms the transitivity of the implication operator.

The above examples only manipulated constants, and were thus propositional. Variables and quantifiers lead to more complicated situations, requiring, in addition to *modus ponens*, another inference rule, particular to predicate calculus, that of generalization. If P is true, we deduce:

V x P(x)

In order to illustrate *modus ponens* on formulae with variables, consider the following facts:

if x is the husband of y, then y is the wife of x;

Emmanuel is the husband of Danielle.

After suitable substitutions of variables, we can deduce that Danielle is the wife of Emmanuel.

The different steps taken by a theorem prover, that is how it makes deductions, are now described.

Normal forms
As for all formal manipulation, the formulae to be considered must be presented in normal form. Automatic deduction programs use clausal form. This is a language even more limited than predicate calculus, since it contains neither ≡ nor =>, nor the existential quantifier. It is, however, more powerful because of its close relationship to normal form.

To translate a formula of predicate calculus into clausal form, it is first necessary to replace existentially quantified variables by constants or by Skolem functions. Thus, existential quantifiers are eliminated. The formula is then rewritten in prenex normal form, bringing all the universal quantifiers to the left of the formula. The next step transforms it to conjunctive normal form, removing the implication and equivalence connectors and applying the rules concerning the operators NOT, & and OR. A formula in conjunctive normal form is the conjunction (AND) of a set of formulae of which each is a disjunction (OR) of possibly negated literals. A literal is a predicate symbol followed by its argument or arguments.

The result of these transformations is a set of clauses of the form:

(L1 OR L2 OR ...) & ... (Li OR Li+1 OR ...) & (Ln OR Ln+1 OR ...)

where each Li is a negative or a positive literal, that is preceded or not by NOT, in which all variables are implicitly universally quantified. Therefore, a clause is a disjunction of literals, and a formula a conjunction of clauses. Those readers familiar with Boolean algebra, or who are familiar with formal manipulation, will recognize the technique. The particular normal form chosen depends on the requirements of the theorem prover, and, in particular, whether it aims at proving or refuting hypotheses. Refutation is the more frequently used technique.

A proof applies to a hypothesis, which is to be confirmed or refuted from a set of known facts (axioms or established deductions). This reduces to proving a formula of the following type:

F1 & F2 & ... & Fn => H

where the Fi are known facts and H the hypothesis in question. Working by refutation means transforming this into a set of clauses which refute the hypothesis:

F1 & F2 & ... & Fn & NOT H

With this form, the prover looks for a contradiction, deducing from F1, F2 ... Fn, NOT H in a certain number of steps, new clauses. Deduction stops when a clause is produced which is in direct contradiction with given or deduced facts. This can only come from NOT H, since the Fi are already known to be true. If a contradiction is found, the hypothesis is true. Mathematically inclined readers will recognize the technique of *reductio ad absurdum*.

The following algorithm generates clausal normal form by the application of a sequence of steps carried out on a formula from predicate calculus:

1: Close the formula by adding the quantifier THEREEXISTS for each free variable, then the system will try to prove that there cannot exist any x such that the formula is TRUE. Adding THEREEXISTS prepares the search for a contradiction. For example, consider the formula F1:

F1: $\forall$ (y) (wife(y,x) & husband(x,y) => married(y,x))

This reads 'for all y, if y is the wife of x and x is the husband of y, then x and y are married'. It is translated into the formula F2 by adding the existential quantifier for the free variable, as follows:

F2: $\forall$ (y) THEREEXISTS(x) (wife)(y,x) & husband(x,y) => married(y,x))

2: Elimination of => and $\equiv$ by application of the definitions given previously. Formula F2 is transformed into F3:

F3: $\forall$ (y) THEREEXISTS(x) (NOT(wife(y,x) & husband(x,y)) OR married(y,x))

3: Occurrences of NOT are brought as far inside the formula as possible by application of de Morgan's law. For example, F3 is transformed into F4:

F4: $\forall$ (y) THEREEXISTS(x) (NOT wife(y,x) OR NOT husband(x,y) OR married(y,x))

4: If two variables have the same name, one of them is renamed.
5: The quantifier THEREEXISTS is eliminated. Each x bound by THEREEXISTS x is replaced by a new variable name. If such an x is in the scope of a $\forall$ y, then the new name is a function of y, called a Skolem function. If the THEREEXISTS precedes the $\forall$, then the existentially quantified variable is replaced by a constant. All occurrences of THEREEXISTS disappear. Intuitively, this transformation names the object which is said to exist. For example:

THEREEXISTS(w) $\forall$(x) $\forall$(y) THEREEXISTS(z) P(w,x,y,z)

becomes $\forall$(x) $\forall$(y) P(a,x,y,f(x,y)), where a is a constant and f a constant function of x and y, universally quatified. F4 becomes F5:

F5: $\forall$ (y) (NOT wife(y,h(y)) OR NOT husband (h(y),y) OR
married(y,h(y)))

where wife(y,h(y)) reads y is the wife of the husband of y. If the THEREEXISTS(x) had been in front of V (y), then x would have been replaced by a constant.

6: The occurrences of V are taken to the outside of the formula. The formula is now in prenex normal form.

7: The formula is rewritten in conjunctive normal form by the application of the rules of distribution of OR over &:

A OR (B & C) becomes (A OR B) & (A OR C)

This form will be familiar to those who have worked with Boolean algebra.

8: Elimination of tautologies. A OR NOT A is eliminated, since always TRUE.

9: Rewrite the formula in the language of set theory. The V disappear, and operators become implicit. For example:

Vz ((P(a) OR P(b)) & (P(a) OR Q(b)) & NOT P(z))

becomes PaPb PaQb NOT Px, where x is a new variable name. The formula is thus transformed into a set of clauses, all of which are disjunctions of literals and in which all variables are universally quantified.

It can be shown that these transformations preserve the essential properties of the formula, that is that the confirmation or refutation of a normalized formula implies that of the original. The theoretical development is not given here.

Resolution

The preparation of formulae by putting them into normal form is done to facilitate the proof process. The result of Herbrand (1930) shows that the process can always be applied. Following this theoretical step, different decision algorithms have been invented. What follows is a presentation of one of these (Davis and Putnam 1960), as it is presented in Loveland (1978). In a later section we give a second, more efficient algorithm.

The Davis-Putnam procedure applies to a set of clauses which constitute a formula in normal form containing only constants (fundamental clauses). It is a series of rules which are applied recursively until a conclusion is found, or until it is seen that the available information is insufficient. The latter case is deduced from the fact that no rule can any longer be applied. The set of rules comprises:

1: Eliminate tautologies.

2: One literal rule. If any clause is made up of just one literal, say L, then L is TRUE. The clause disappears, together with all the occurrences of L in other clauses.

3: Affirmative-negative rule. If the literal L occurs in one or more clauses, but there are no occurrences of NOT L in the formula, then L disappears, as in 2. This happens because we can freely choose the value of L. Since deduction reduces to finding combinations of values (TRUE or FALSE) for the different variables such that the formula is true, the value of L is chosen in this sense. The same technique is applied to a literal which occurs only in the form NOT L, with no occurrence of L.

4: Splitting. When steps 2 or 3 can no longer be applied, consider any literal L in the formula. No clause contains L and NOT L, since that would be a tautology, eliminated by 1. There exist clauses containing L and clauses containing NOT L (see 3). These are separated as follows:
   – one new clause set results from the suppression of all the clauses which contain L together with all occurrences of NOT L in the rest;
   – a second set comes from the suppression of all clauses containing NOT L and all occurrences of L in the rest.

The literal L has disappeared from the formula. This rule gradually eliminates all the literals in the formula.

5: Covering rule. Any clause whose elements are all contained in some other clause is eliminated. For example, consider the following set of clauses:

(A) & (A OR B) & (B OR C)) & (E OR F)

The clause (A OR B) is eliminated, since it is covered by (A), that is that if A is true, A OR B is true whatever the value of B, which is thus irrelevant.

The procedure loops round steps 2 to 5 until a solution is obtained. This is either a contradiction or the disappearence of all the clauses, which is a confirmation. The theory shows that the procedure is sufficient, that is that the original hypothesis is confirmed or refuted if possible. This theoretical result is important for theorem provers, since it justifies their existence. A similar demonstration should be carried out for any new resolution procedure.

Semantic trees

To visualize the deductions which lead to a refutation, trees can again be used. The technique is illustrated by a simple example. Consider the complete tree with three predicates P,Q,R given in Figure 17.

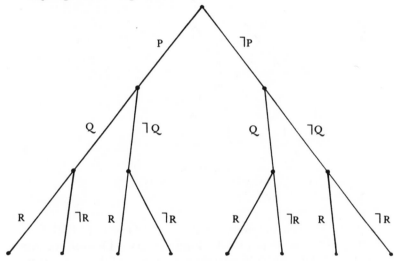

Figure 17.
Complete tree with three predicates

This example, together with certain aspects of what follows, comes from the excellent book by Chang and Lee (1979). The complete binary tree shows, by the different paths from the root to its leaves, all the possible combinations of values TRUE and FALSE that the predicates can take.

Consider now a set of clauses in normal form which apply to the three predicates:

(P, QR, NOT P NOT Q, NOT P NOT R)

It will be shown that this set cannot be satisfied. The clauses are considered individually, starting from the left. The first clause says that P is TRUE. Thus, NOT P is FALSE, which cuts off the set of paths which include NOT P. These constitute a sub-tree of Figure 17. Figure 18 shows the result of the cut.

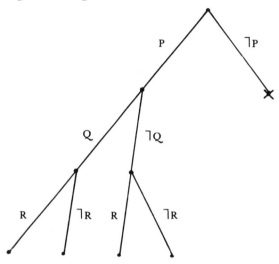

Figure 18.
Closure of the branch NOT P

Similarly, the clause QR says that one of Q or R is TRUE. If Q is FALSE, then R is TRUE, and vice versa. This cuts off the path P, NOT Q, NOT R. Applying the rest of the constraints in the same way leads to the tree shown in Figure 19.

Since the application of the set of clauses has completely closed the tree, this means that no path can exist from the root to a leaf. A completely closed tree corresponds to an unsatisfiable formula, that is that the underlying hypothesis is refuted.

In the above example, the predicates had no parameters. When these exist, the process is more complicated, but the principle remains the same. Some examples of parameter manipulation are found in the following section.

General resolution and unification
The first resolution algorithms were based on truth tables. They were relatively slow, as is the Davis-Putnam algorithm given above. As long as they were not required to be used too

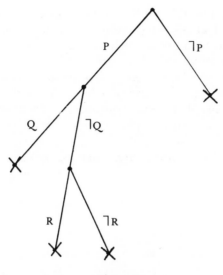

Figure 19.
Reduced tree

frequently, this was not a serious problem, but the arrival of expert systems meant that they needed improvement. An expert system calls the theorem prover frequently, and the reaction time is an important factor in the evaluation of performance. An important step was taken with the work on unification. and resolution which started with Robinson (1965).

The principle of general resolution is an extension of the splitting rule of Davis and Putnam. Consider the following two clauses presented in a rule on page 63:

P OR Q   NOT P OR R

If P is TRUE, then R is also TRUE, and if P is FALSE, then Q is TRUE. Combining these two results leads to the elimination of P and the creation of what is called the resolvant, in this case the clause:

Q OR R

The resolvant is the logical conclusion of the combination of the two clauses. The process is possible whatever the number of terms in the clauses as long as one of them contains a positive occurrence of a literal and the other a negative occurrence of the same literal. Q OR R represents the union of the remaining terms in the two clauses after elimination of P in the one and NOT P in the other.

Resolvants are added to the set of available clauses, which augment the number of facts which can be used in the rest of the proof. Consider for example the problem considered in Figures 17 to 19 where the semantic tree showed that the formula could not be satisfied. The set of clauses is presented here with the OR explicitly indicated, to make them easier to read:

1) P
2) Q OR R
3) NOT P OR NOT Q
4) NOT P OR NOT R

The following resolvants can be deduced:

5) NOT Q   (1+3)
6) NOT R   (1+4)
7) R   (2+5)
8) NIL (the empty clause)   (6+7)

The deduction of the empty clause as a resolvant is an indication of a contradiction.

Resolution can also be expressed in terms of trees. Figure 20 shows the refutation tree for the considered example. The leaves of this upside-down tree (ie the right way up in normal languages) have been reordered so as to facilitate the drawing of the diagram. Its interpretation is obvious.

The above examples had no parameters, which avoids one of the major problems. A predicate applied to constants is itself a constant. The variables lead to difficulties. Consider the following two clauses:

1) P(x) OR Q(x)
2) NOT P(f(y)) OR R(y)

x and y are variables, f a function. The problem is to find suitable values of substitution for x,y and f(y), so that

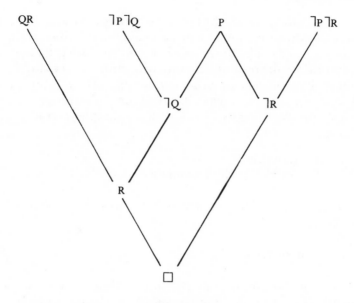

Figure 20.
Refutation tree

resolution can be carried out. One possibility is to replace y by the constant a and x by f(a), which leads to:

1) P(f(a)) OR l(f(a))
2) Not P(f(a)) OR R(a)

The resolvant is thus:

Q(f(a)) OR R(a)

In fact, the chosen substitution was too strong, since the constant need not be fixed at this point. A minimal substitution would be the replacement of x by f(y), which leads to the resolvant:

Q(f(y)) OR R(y)

Note that variable names can be changed as long as consistency is maintained. The implicit quantifier takes charge of these name substitutions.

These substitutions, which transform the parameters of

77

predicates to allow resolution, are examples of the technique called unification. Two literals are said to be unified if there exists a way of substituting variables in each such that, after substitution, the resulting literals are identical except for their signs. The process of unification must always allow the discovery of the most general satisfactory substitution which makes the two literals identical. For example, consider the clauses:

woman (charlotte)
NOT man(x) OR NOT woman(x)

They contain literals that can be unified to produce the resolvant:

NOT man(charlotte)

by the substitution of x by charlotte and the suppression of literals of opposite sign (women(charlotte) and NOT woman(charlotte)).

Other examples are given on page 115, as part of the presentation of PROLOG. There exists a general unification algorithm (in fact several) which allows general resolution. The algorithm is not presented here.

An example
The following example illustrates the normalization of a formula of predicate calculus and the general principles of resolution. It is inspired by a puzzle published by a popular magazine (J&S 1984b) which has been largely modified. The proof technique follows the style of Wos *et al.* (1984).

The problem concerns five people called Arthur, Bernard, Claude, David and Eric, respectively. Each has a different profession, either musician, navigator, officer, professor or reporter. They are linked by family ties, as follows:

1) The musician is the grandfather of the officer.
2) Bernard is the father of Arthur.
3) Eric is the father of the professor.
4) The reporter is the father of the navigator.
5) David is the father of Claude.

Given that all the personalities are inveterate liars, the problem is to find each one's profession from the following hypotheses (which are all false because they all lie):

1) Arthur: If I am an officer, then Claude is a musician.
2) Bernard: If I am a professor, then Eric is an officer.
3) Claude: If I am not an officer, then Arthur is a navigator.
4) David: If I am a reporter, then Eric is a professor.
5) Eric: If I am not a navigator, then Bernard is an officer.

Since all the propositions are false, they must all be negated. In the formulae which follow, names and professions are represented by their first letters and A(x,y) represents the fact that person x has activity y. The implications are as follows:

NOT (A(a,o) => A(c,m))
NOT (A(b,p) => A(e,o))
NOT ((NOT A(c,o)) => A(a,n))
NOT (A(d,r) => A(e,p))
NOT ((NOT A(e,n)) => A(b,o))

These formulae can be transformed into clausal form by a number of steps.

REMOVING THE IMPLICATIONS
As was seen in the section on normal forms (see page 68), a first step towards clausal form is the suppression of the implication operator. The rule is:

P => Q

is replaced by NOT P OR Q. At the same time, we replace NOT NOT P by P. This leads to:
   NOT ((NOT A(a,o)) OR A(c,m))
   NOT ((NOT A(b,p)) OR A(e,o))
   NOT (A(c,o) OR A(a,n))
   NOT ((NOT A(d,r)) OR A(e,p))
   NOT (A(e,n) OR A(b,o))

CONJUNCTIVE NORMAL FORM
The different occurrences of NOT are taken inside the formula by the rule which replaces:

NOT (P OR Q)

by (NOT P) & (NOT Q). Double negatives are again eliminated:

A(a,o) & NOT A(c,m)
A(b,p) & NOT A(e,o)
NOT A(c,o) & NOT A(a,n)
A(d,r) & NOT A(e,p)
NOT A(e,n) & NOT A(b,o)

These five formulae are implicitly linked by &.

CLAUSAL FORM
Each of the above formulae is, in fact, a pair of one-literal clauses linked by &. Separating the pairs leads to the following set of 10 independent clauses, all linked implicitly by &.

1) A(a,o)
2) NOT A(c,m)
3) A(b,p)
4) NOT A(e,o)
5) NOT A(c,o)
6) NOT A(a,n)
7) A(d,r)
8) NOT A(e,p)
9) NOT A(e,n)
10) NOT A(b,o)

Clause 1 reads 'a is an o' ('arthur is an officer'), clause 2 'c is not an m' ('claude is not a musician') and so on. At a human level, the set allows the following deductions:

 - Arthur is an officer (1).
 - Bernard is a professor (3).
 - Claude is neither musician (2) nor officer (5).
 - David is a reporter (7).
 - Eric is not an officer (4), neither is he a professor (8), nor a navigator (9).

This information is sufficient for the human problem solver to deduce that Claude is a navigator (somebody must be, and nobody else can be), and that Eric is a musician (the last available profession). The theorem prover cannot make these deductions because it has as yet no means of eliminating possibilities, since formalization is not yet complete. Elimination is difficult to mechanize at the level of logic used.

Therefore, the reader will have realized that the problem can be solved without using the given family relationships. They will, nevertheless, be used in the formal proof, first to get round the elimination difficulty, and second to demonstrate more manipulation techniques.

Note that, although human problem solvers do not need to go into all the details of the mechanization process, a knowledge of the above basic principles is of considerable help in solving problems. A mathematician could find the above solution very quickly by the simple use of algebra.

FAMILY RELATIONSHIPS
The problem statement contained the following information concerning family relationships:

1) If x is an officer and y his grandfather, then y is a musician.
2) Bernard is Arthur's father.
3) If x is a professor, then Eric is his father.
4) If x is a reporter, and the father of y, then y is a navigator.
5) David is Claude's father.

Translating these relationships into clausal form, and eliminating implications by the usual substitution, leads to the following clauses, in which GF stands for grandfather and F for father:

11 NOT A(x,o) OR NOT GF(y,x) OR A(y,m)
12 F(b,a)
13 NOT A(x,p) OR F(e,x)
14 NOT A(x,r) OR NOT F(x,y) OR A(y,n)
15 F(d,c)
16 NOT F(x,y) OR NOT F(y,z) OR GF(x,z)

The last clause indicates that a grandfather is a father's father.

To solve the problem requires the introduction of a number of facts which are implicit in the problem statement. A human being does not need an explicit statement that, for example, Bernard, Claude … are names of people, that musician, navigator ... are names of professions, and so on. The following set of clauses defines the members of the universe, with H representing human being and P profession:

17 H(a)
18 H(b)
19 H(c)
20 H(d)
21 H(e)
22 P(m)
23 P(n)
24 P(o)
25 P(p)
26 P(r)

We need to tell the system that each object in the universe is either a human being or a profession, but not both. This is written in predicate calculus as follows:

$\forall (x) (H(x) => NOT\ P(x))$
$\forall (x) (NOT\ H(X) => P(x))$

This leads to the two clauses:

27 NOT H(x) OR NOT P(x)
28 H(x) OR P(x)

We could also explain that each person has an activity and that each activity is carried out by somebody:

$\forall (x)\ THEREEXISTS(y)\ (H(x) => A(x,y))$
$\forall (y)\ THEREEXISTS(x)\ (P(y) => A(x,y))$

To translate these formulae into clausal form requires replacement of the existentially qualified variables by Skolem functions (see page 68). New functions of universally quantified variables are introduced, the quantifiers being left out as usual. J(x) says that the job occupied by x depends on who is x, and O(y) says that the occupant of job y depends on which job it is. The new clauses are:

29 NOT H(x) OR A(x,J(x))
30 NOT P(y) OR A(O(y),y)

These clauses are introduced as an example of Skolemization. They will not be used in the proof.

The system needs to know that people and professions with different names are different entities. We introduce predicates EH ('equal humans') and EP (equal professions). They are negated in all the possible combinations. The following clauses suppose that the quality predicates are symmetrical, otherwise they would need repetition with the parameters in the opposite oder:

```
31  NOT EH(a,b)
32  NOT EH(a,c)
33  NOT EH(a,d)
34  NOT EH(a,e)
35  NOT EH(b,c)
36  NOT EH(b,d)
37  NOT EH(b,e)
38  NOT EH(c,d)
39  NOT EH(c,e)
40  NOT EH(d,e)
41  NOT EP(m,n)
42  NOT EP(m,o)
43  NOT EP(m,p)
44  NOT EP(m,r)
45  NOT EP(n,o)
46  NOT EP(n,p)
47  NOT EP(n,r)
48  NOT EP(o,p)
49  NOT EP(o,r)
50  NOT EP(p,r)
```

Finally, we need two rules which show that the same person cannot have two different professions and that two different people cannot have the same profession:

(NOT EP(y,z) & A(x,y)) => NOT A(x,z)
(NOT EH(x,z) AND A(x,y)) => NOT A(z,y)

In the usual way, these become:

```
51  EP(y,z) OR NOT A(x,y) OR NOT A(x,z)
52  EH(x,z) OR NOT A(x,y) OR NOT A(z,y)
```

RESOLUTION

From clauses 1, 3 and 7, the professions of Arthur, Bernard and David are known. Therefore, there remain two unknowns, which are the professions of Claude and Eric. We start with Eric.

Clauses 4, 8 and 9 showed that Eric is not an officer, neither is he a professor or a navigator. He is thus a reporter or a musician. Since clause 7 says that David is a reporter, we can deduce that Eric is a musician, but the mechanical proof remains to be done. We work by contradiction.

The method proceeds by steps which, from a set of facts and rules, deduce new facts, which are added to the set, until a contradiction is found. The contradiction can only come from the negation of the hypothesis, which is included in the set of known facts. In the present example, the clause which we wish to prove is:

53 NOT A(e,r)

Its opposite is thus included in the set of facts:

53' A(e,r)

The clauses which allow this proof are the following:

53' A(e,r)
7   A(d,r)
40   NOT EH(d,e)
52   EH(x,z) OR NOT A(x,y) OR NOT A(z,y)

The deduction program takes pairs of literals which can be unified and carries out substitutions to make the unification possible. The substitution/unification process (called S/U from here on) allows resolution (R). S/U and R are steps in the proof process which follows:

I	EH(d,z) OR NOT A(d,r) OR NOT A(z,r)	By S/U on 7+52
II	EH(d,z) OR NOT A(z,r)	R on I+7
III	EH(d,e) OR NOT A(e,r)	S/U on 40+II
IV	NOT A(e,r)	R on 40+III
V	NIL (contradiction)	R on 53'+IV

I.   Unification of clauses 7 and 52 after substitution of d for x and r for y.

II.   Clause 7 says A(d,r) is TRUE, and thus resolution with I leads the suppression of the opposite literal NOT A(d,r) in I. II is thus the resolvant of 7 and I.

III.   Substitution of z by e leads to the unification of clauses 40 and II.

IV.   And the corresponding resolution removes the literal EH(d,e).

V.   The clauses 53' and IV are in direct contradiction. Their resolvant is the empty clause NIL. The supposition A(e,r) is thus in contradiction with the known facts. We have thus proved this supposition false, and hence:

53   NOT A(e,r)

This proof could have been obtained in various other ways, for example from 52 and 40.

Eric is thus not an officer, not a professor, not a navigator and not a reporter. Therefore, he is a musician, but once again this needs to be proved. This uses the clauses 1, 3, 11, 12, 13 and 16 and the negation of A(e,m) as supposition. In fact, we know by 11 that the grandfather of the officer is a musician, by 1 that Arthur is an officer, by 12 that Bernard is the father of Arthur, by 13 that Eric is the father of the professor and by 3 that Bernard is the professor. This leads to:

```
1    A(a,o)
3    A(b,p)
11   NOT A(x,o) OR NOT GF(y,x) OR A(y,m)
12   F(b,a)
13   NOT A(x,p) OR F(e,x)
16   NOT F(x,y) OR NOT F(x,y) OR GF(x,z)
54'  NOT A(e,m)
```

We obtain:

I	NOT A(b,p) OR F(e,b)	S/U on 13+3
II	F(e,b)	R on 3+I
III	NOT F(x,b) OR NOT F(b,a) OR	
	GF(x,a)	S/U on 12+16

IV	NOT F(e,b) OR NOT F(b,a) OR	
	GF(e,a)	S/U on II+III
V	GF(e,a)	R on II+12+IV
VI	NOT A(a,o) OR NOT GF(y,a) OR	
	A(y,m)	S/U on 11+1
VII	NOT A(a,o) OR NOT GF(e,a) OR	
	A(e,m)	S/U on V+VI
VIII	A(e,m)	R on 1+V+VII
IX	NIL	R on 54'+VIII

The hypothesis NOT A(e,m) leads to a contradiction. It is therefore false, and we can deduce the verity of:

54 A(e,m)

Moving on now to the case of Claude, we know by 2 and 5 that he is neither musician nor officer. We leave the proofs that he is neither professor nor reporter as exercises for the reader (use 3 and 7). He is thus a navigator, as can be seen from the following set of clauses:

55' NOT A(c,n)
7   A(d,r)
14 NOT A(x,r) OR NOT F(x,y) OR A(y,n)
15 F(d,c)

The deduction is in the usual style:

I	NOT A(d,r) OR NOT F(d,y) OR	
	A(y,n)	S/U on 14+7
II	NOT F(d,y) OR A(y,n)	R on 7+I
III	NOT F(d,c) OR A(c,n)	S/U on 15+II
IV	A(c,n)	R on 15+III
V	NIL	Ron 55'+IV

Since NOT A(c,n) leads to a contradiction, we have indeed proved that Claude is a navigator.

CONCLUSION
Examples of this type, although artificial, show up many of the characteristics of theorem provers. The number of steps is usually large, and the amount of information required is considerable.

In the above treatment, we have given only the set of productive and necessary steps. In the computer, other calculations would have been made. The efficiency of proof depends on the theorem prover itself, whether its strategy is sufficiently directed towards the goal, and on the order in which information is given. Goal-directed proof strategy is an important field of research. In general, the user will not know the optimum order in which to write rules, but the prover will apply unification and resolution to pairs of clauses in some order. Experienced users will thus benefit more quickly than inexperienced ones.

This example is given as an exercise in PROLOG at the end of Chapter 6. A programmed solution is given in Appendix 2. Knowledge of PROLOG influenced the presentation of the example, which confirms that using the language is a help towards understanding automated theorem proving.

Synthesis
Automated theorem proving has been dreamed of by mathematicians for hundreds of years. Herbrand's 1930 work is a landmark in the field. It gives a refutation algorithm which after a certain time otherwise (semi-solvable). Church (1936) and Turing (1936) show that the semi-resolvable property is a limit. With the arrival of computers, it was natural to program these already existing algorithms, which led to the first generation of useful provers.

The work of Robinson (1965, 1979), briefly described above, made the process much more efficient. There has followed a considerable volume of research, and the subject is still very topical. There now exists a variety of provers, with different types of logic. These research developments came in time to allow expert systems to work reasonably well. Chapter 5 shows how expert systems use theorem provers, and to what extent the work outlined above is applicable to different fields.

Expert systems

It is with the arrival of expert systems that artificial intelligence is being introduced into many fields. Instead of remaining a separate esoteric discipline, it has become a necessity which qualitatively improves the performance of application programs.

As was explained in Chapter 1, an expert system stores information. Using this, it makes decisions which ought to be the same as those that would be taken by a human being who is an expert in the field. This decision making capacity requires three components:

1) A set of facts which describe the considered universe. They are provided by an expert from the application field.
2) A problem definition which acts as a question. It usually includes supplementary facts, together with a hypothesis (or a set of hypotheses), which is (or are) to be confirmed or rejected. It is the end user who puts these questions.
3) A program which is capable of drawing conclusions from sets of facts by the application of rules. The program is a theorem prover which accepts or rejects the given hypothesis, thus replying to the question which was asked. A general theorem prover can handle different universes, that is be the basis of different expert systems. It simply applies mathematical logic to sets of known facts, as described in Chapter 4.

The three components will be illustrated by the couples problem described on page 49.

Back to a problem

The problem arose from a small party of four couples. At any given moment in time, four conversations take place, under the following conditions:

$$t(B,E) \quad t(A,h(C)) \quad t(w(G),F) \quad t(D,h(A)) \quad t(w(E),G)$$

The question asked is who talks to H. Within the conditions, t is a two-parameter function 'talk together', w the function 'wife of' and h the function 'husband of'. Proper names are replaced by their initials, in capital letters. The woman's name is always written first in relations. The five conditions, together with the question who is talking to H, are the particular problem put to the expert system by an end user.

However, the user's problems is stated within the context of a given universe, whose rules must also be defined. The definition of the basic rules of the game, which represent the common universe, are done once for all by the expert in the field. The universe of the problem contains the definitions of what is a person, a marriage, or a conversation, together with the definitions of the functions used in the question. In particular, at least the following rules are needed:

1) Each person is married once and only once.
2) Marriages are between one man and one woman.
3) The above two rules apply also to conversations (in the particular world studied).
4) The functions w and h must be defined, and in particular their interactions with the definition of marriage.

The universe must be formalized, which could lead to rules of the following type:

$$m(x,y) \;\&\; m(x,z) => y=z$$
$$m(x,y) \;\&\; m(z,y) => x=z$$
$$t(x,y) \;\&\; t(x,z) => y=z$$
$$t(x,y) \;\&\; t(z,y) => x=z$$

(marriages and conversations are monogamous).

$$m(A,E) \text{ OR } m(A,F) \text{ OR } m(A,G) \text{ OR } m(A,H)$$
$$m(B,E) \text{ OR } m(B,F) \text{ OR } m(B,G) \text{ OR } m(B,H)$$
$$m(C,E) \text{ OR } m(C,F) \text{ OR } m(C,G) \text{ OR } m(C,H)$$

m(D,E) OR m(D,F) OR m(D,G) OR m(D,H)
(each woman is married, monogamy implying that each man is also).

t(A,E) OR t(A,F) OR t(A,G) OR t(A,H)
t(B,E) OR t(B,F) OR t(B,G) OR t(B,H)
t(C,E:) OR t(C,F) OR t(C,G) OR t(C,H)
t(D,E) OR t(D,F) OR t(D,G) OR t(D,H)
(the same thing is true for conversations).

$x=w(y) <=> m(x,y) <=> y=h(x)$
(implications of the defined relations).

To solve the given problem in its defined universe, the above sets of rules must be given to a theorem prover. It would find, within the limits shown up in Chapter 4, and after a certain time, the solution given on page 53. The prover combines the given rules in order to choose which of the possible hypotheses is TRUE. It will try to confirm or reject successively the four different possibilities:

t(A,H)   t(B,H)   t(C,H)   t(D,H)

The theorem prover looks like those considered in Chapter 4, which use the axioms of first order logic, or possibly more sophisticated methods.

This example is completely artificial, since it is difficult to imagine the construction of an expert system to solve the set of problems about couples. However, it does allow a presentation of the three principle components given previously. Each of these will now be looked at separately.

Making expert systems
The problem here is that of writing the set of rules which describe the universe, like that of marriages and conversations above. The universe defines the field inside which questions can be put. For practical applications, this can mean analysing parts of medicine, organic chemistry, the topology of placing circuits on a chip, or any part of human knowledge which it is required to automate or to model.

The analysis of an application field in order to formalize its rules is an extremely difficult task. The ordinary professional is not capable of a sufficient degree of self-analysis. In particular, not everybody is conscious, with the necessary precision, of the underlying principles of his own profession. The experts must, therefore, be a recognized authority. His problems are of various kinds, from the need to formalize, for computing reasons, to the intrinsic difficulty of making explicit the sum total of all the knowledge accumulated by professional experience.

To master the necessary formalism, it is usual for a computer specialist to pair with an expert from the application field. There is now a new profession emerging in the field of computing, that of knowledge engineer. During numerous discussion and work sessions, he helps an expert to extract and code the rules established in a particular field. It should be noted that the knowledge engineer cannot do the job himself. He must serve as the catalyst to force the expert to give all the available information in a usable form. The major effort in a given discipline is made by the expert.

We have stressed the difficulty of the expert's job. Consider the example of a system for medical diagnosis, which is currently a privileged field for the introduction of expert systems. It could be thought that the rules are merely transcriptions of the best books on the subject, but this is not so. The information they contain is not organized in a way which allows coding using formal rules, and doctors are not, in fact, in agreement over the details of the process. There is no determinist definition of many illnesses and, above all, much professional knowledge is held in non-explicit rules of the type 'everybody knows that'. This last point is most important, and is the source of many difficulties. Returning to the couples problem, all the information about marriages and conversations is implicit for a human solver, but needs formal coding for a theorem prover. In many fields, the quantity of information is large, and experts find it difficult to do a complete job.

What is more, a practical doctor often uses a variable technique. When he sees a pimply child with a temperature, his attitude may well be influenced by an epidemic of chicken pox in town. Giving all the real rules is a long-term process.

The role of the knowledge engineer, who is usually an expert in computing, but may originate from a field such as psychology, is a delicate one. There are real dangers in situations where the wrong person may be taking decisions.

The knowledge engineer should not have to learn the rules of the expert's field, and should certainly not make any decision within the field. In the same way, the expert must say what he really wants, and not try to simplify 'in order to ease the computer's job'. We are, in general, opposed to the current trend of creating specialists with dual competence, which means teaching doctors, for example, with enough computing to make them independent. While this solution may be right for certain application programs, it is usually insufficient when complex systems are required. With rare exceptions, dual competence specialists are usually less competent than they should be in at least one of their two fields (and often in both).

In practice, the inspection of a field of knowledge by experts can provoke reflection within the discipline. One can imagine that doctors will slowly change some of their habits with the installation of expert diagnostic systems. This by no means implies that programs will replace doctors in the foreseeable future. The latter will remain the masters in their own house, as must the practitioners of all the fields which will use expert systems. For medicine, some of the moral and philosophical questions are considered in Shortliffe (1976). Computer specialists are not to decide the future of other fields.

CODING THE KNOWLEDGE BASE

The set of rules, produced by an expert, which describes his field of knowledge, is called the knowledge base of the expert system. In many experimental systems, the knowledge base was coded in computer readable form by the knowledge engineer, after interrogation of the expert. This is not the best solution, since it may introduce errors due to false interpretations by the knowledge engineer, whose understanding of the described subject is often, at best, limited.

A greater degree of security is obtained when the expert can read the coded rules, and even more so if he can write them. Since it is not reasonable to ask him to become a computer specialist, he needs a friendly interface to help him in this task. This interface is necessarily particular to the field described, and is used essentially only by the expert, or, after the system has been installed, by maintenance engineers. It can seem expensive to create for the amount of time used, but it is, nevertheless, essential if we are to produce reliable long-term systems.

In fact, in future systems, the expert interface will be used over a long period of time. The idea of a fixed knowledge base, created at the introduction of the system and unchanged afterwards, results from the fact that current expert systems are often prototypes of limited application. As systems are created to model extensive knowledge domains, the knowledge bases will grow as experience in using them is acquired.

Note that the expert interface is different from the user interface, which allows end users to interrogate the knowledge base. The user interface is studied later.

Although different formalizations have been tried, the most common interface structure is that of the IF clause. The expert writes rules in the form:

IF Predicate
THEN Deduction

The predicate can be any formula of first order logic, the deduction being a new fact to be added to the knowledge base if the predicate is true. Of course, the deduction is only valid during the solution of a particular problem, in which the predicate is true. Simple examples of this form could be:

IF it is raining
THEN the ground is damp

or:

IF temp > 99
THEN fever

In general, predicates tend to be more complex than these examples, using combinations of clauses with no connectives such as AND and OR. This form is easily translated into formulae for the theorem prover. Thus:

IF P THEN D

translates to:

P=> D

AN EXAMPLE

An early program used in the production of medical diagnostic systems was MYCIN, already referenced (Shortliffe 1976). It contained a conversational rule acquisition system which guides the expert, as in the example from the book given in Program 9.

```
**NR
The new rule will be called RULE200.
If:   1 **THE ORGANISM IS A GRAM NEGATIVE ROD
and   2 **IT IS ANAEROBIC
and   3 **IT WAS ISOLATED FROM THE BLOOD
and   4 **YOU THINK THE PORTAL WAS THE GI TRACT
and   5 **
Then: 1 **IT IS PROBABLY A BACTEROIDES
      On a scale of 1 to 10, how much certainty would you
      affix to this conclusion?
      **9
and   2 **
```

Program 9
Input of a MYCIN rule

The user gave the information written in capital letters after **, a carriage return indicating the end of data input in the category. NR indicates that the rule is a new one. The result is stored by MYCIN in LISP.

The expert receives a summary of the rule in the form that would be presented to an end user asking for information (see page 96). The difficulty in this method comes from the need to analyse conditions and results by some sort of keyword analysis of natural language (in fact, pseudo-natural).

As the reader can see, this type of expert interface can be applied to a large number of different situations. It is thus possible to have a general structure for interfaces, which needs extensions to take into account particular points in the field to be considered.

Using expert systems

The user of an expert system is a normal practitioner in his field. He has no particular competence in computing, and has probably never had to formalize his problems. A reasonable estimate of the time he will agree to spend in learning a new system varies from a few hours to a few days. At the end of this learning period, he must be able to use the system with immediate benefit, without having to make frequent references to the documentation, which in any case must be limited in volume.

This means that the interface of an expert system must be user friendly. In particular, it must be accessible in a language which is close to that normally used in the field under consideration. The architecture of the interface is a job for the expert, preferably after consultation with colleagues, since they alone know what can or cannot be written. But it must be constructed by computer professionals. The work required to produce adequate interfaces has been largely underestimated, and the same is true for the level of difficulty of the task. Before finishing the design, final users must also be consulted, since experts tend not to understand the difficulties that junior colleagues sometimes encounter.

Current work on natural languages, or on sub-languages, for these interfaces should be interesting, but the current state of the art does not allow the construction of generalized interpreters of natural language. Even if this were possible, their use would lead to other problems. The interfaces to different expert systems have to be constructed independently.

The are different aspects to consider in an interface. The most obvious is the form in which problems are presented, including the information given about the particular problem as well as the question itself. The ease of understanding of results is an equally obvious criterion, but we must also consider the degree of help that the system supplies. This is of two forms. The first is the standard aid familiar to users of microcomputers, which is an on-line documentary system. The second is the justification or explanation of the proposed decision. If the user wishes, he ought to be able to inspect the chain of reasoning used by the system to get to its conclusion.

THE USER INTERFACE

MYCIN is a good illustration of a user interface. However, any description would run to several pages, which can already be found in Shortliffe (1976). We give only a summary of its design points and one example of a printout of a MYCIN rule.

A consultation session requires the conversational exchange of an important amount of information. After an initial dialogue which identifies the patient and gives the basic facts about him, such as sex, age, etc., the consultant selects an application field. A new dialogue establishes the facts known by the consultant, during which time the system asks those questions whose answers enable it to reach a conclusion. This is presented to the consultant in a suitable form.

Among the design criteria were usefulness, ability to evolve, modifiability, ability to explain and the use of natural language. Usefulness is a general system criterion which we will not discuss. Evolution and modification are facilitated by the expert interface. Explanations are given whenever the user asks for them. These take the form of a list of the rules applied, together with the partial solutions they allowed. The contents of the rules themselves can be given in a semi-natural form. For example, if the rule on page 97 was given, it would take the form of Program 10.

```
RULE200
IF:  1) THE SITE OF THE CULTURE IS BLOOD, AND
     2) THE STAIN OF THE ORGANISM IS GRAMNEG, AND
     3) THE MORPHOLOGY OF THE ORGANISM IS ROD, AND
     4) THE AEROBICITY OF THE ORGANISM IS ANAEROBIC, AND
     5) THE PORTAL OF ENTRY OF THE ORGANISM IS GI
THEN THERE  IS STRONGLY SUGGESTIVE EVIDENCE (.9)  THAT  THE
     IDENTITY OF THE ORGANISM IS BACTEROIDES
```

Progam 10.
Printout of a MYCIN rule

User interfaces are necessarily more particular than expert interfaces. They are also more heavily used, and by less competent people. They must be convivial and reliable as well as being easy to learn.

Theorem prover
The theorem prover of an expert system follows the scheme given in Chapter 4. But the intensive use necessary in an expert system, the need for efficiency and the increasing variety of questions have stimulated research on different aspects. In fact, the quantity of work in universities has led to too many people working on theorem provers, and not enough on the construction of practical expert systems. Since theorem proving has a more theoretical basis, this academic preference is understandable, and it must be admitted that considerable progress has been made in a short period of time.

Some degree of agreement has been reached on basic

strategies of proof, which are considered in the next section. Other topis are still subject to research, and we will simply give some idea of current directions in a subsequent section.

PROOF STRATEGY
An important first distinction lies in the direction of deduction. The terms used are forward and backward chaining. A proof is the construction of a deduction tree which associates a hypothesis with a subset of the set of known facts (those which are required in the proof). As in syntax analysis, the relation between premisses and a conclusion is established by production rules. These are the rules given by the expert. Given a production rule of the form:

IF p1 & p2 & ... pn THEN C

its application gives rise to a sub-tree of the form given in Figure 21.

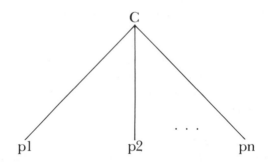

Figure 21.
Deduction sub-tree

A complete proof gives rise to a tree in which the root is the hypothesis to be proved and the leaves are initial facts. Intermediate nodes represent constituent deductions of the above type. Thus, the pi of the example could be the conclusions of other production rules.

The terms forward and backward chaining refer to the

direction in which the tree is constructed. Starting with the hypothesis H, the system can search for a rule of the form:

IF a1 & a2 & ... ap THEN H

This means that if all the ai are known facts, then the hypothesis is proven. If the values of some of the ai are not yet know, then they are treated as sub-goals, to be proved by the same mechanism. This is known as backward chaining, and resembles a bottom-up method of syntax analysis.

Creating the tree in the opposite order resembles top-down syntax analysis, and is called forward chaining. Given the set of known facts, the system combines them by using the production rules to deduce new facts, which are added to the set. It will look for a rule of the form:

IF a1 & a2 & ... ap THEN C

for which all the ai are known facts. C is the a fact to add to the set of known facts. The process is complete when H is the deduction to be drawn from the application of a rule of this type.

Each method has its adepts, its advantages and its disadvantages. Systems may use one or the other method, or have some mixed strategy. Mixed strategies have an obvious tendency towards looping, which must be specifically foreseen in the inference engine.

DIRECTIONS OF RESEARCH

In this text we indicate some of the problems that are being studied in research laboratories. To make a more detailed study, the reader will need to consult the specialist literature published in different journals. As can be imagined, there is a large amount published.

At least three research directions can be identified: theoretical foundations, improvements in strategy and the use of proposed conclusions. Each of these is considered separately.

Most systems start with first order logic shown in Chapter 4. This is a natural step since it is the base of traditional logic, which comes to us from Ancient Greece, and it is also common to all systems of mathematical proof. But human beings use other types of reasoning, such as analogy. Current research is exploring the possibilities offered by these methods of reasoning, trying to separate those which could be useful in expert systems.

To give some idea of this kind of work, consider the question of analogy. It has obvious applications in fields such as law, where jurisprudence consists of rules such as 'the last time that a court considered a case similar to this one the decision was...' This is the logic of analogy, incorporated into systems such as ARCHES (Chouraqui 1981). There are, however, obvious disadvantages. Analogy can lead to incorrect conclusions, as in the standard example which compares the moon and a tennis ball. Both of them being round and of the same colour, it can be wrongly deduced that their other properties are the same. This problem will occur in any system of incomplete logic, but the experience is of considerable interest, with evaluation still to be carried out.

Other elements which can be included are those concerning time, for example, which consider dynamic factors in a field which has been static up till now. Another direction is that of modal logic, which includes the ideas of possibility and necessity as built-in connectors.

The first theorem provers were used sparingly, since the number of theorems to prove was small. In expert systems, provers are heavily used, which means that efficiency has become an important factor. Proofs must be driven by adequate strategies. Instead of combining existing theorems in arbitrary order, goals are separated out. These are reduced to sub-goals, and so on, until a goal can be proved directly. Work in this field employs heuristics, together with sophisticated mathematical techniques.

Another field of exploration is that of the degree of certitude that can be attached to information. By the type of logic used, or by writing specific rules, conclusions can be drawn which contain contradictions. Their resolution will be left to the user. It is possible to help him by including conversational possibilities. Medical diagnosis is of this type. A patient with a headache may suffer from, amongst other things, migraine or a brain tumour. In some systems, probabilities may be included by the expert, which are used by the system to take the most likely solution. This would be unfortunate in medicine where, although migraine is much more frequent, the test for a brain tumour must be carried out because of its seriousness.

In practice, the system must retain both possibilities, and it may well propose further tests to be carried out in order to clarify the situation. The choice of test goes along with the idea of choosing a sub-goal of the type 'if I knew the answer to question x, I would be able to solve the problem under consideration'.

Of course, this brief description of research topics in a rapidly evolving field can only give a small idea of the complete scene. One last important idea, which has the merit of informing to some extent the user on the internal working of the theorem prover, is the possibility of clarifying replies by showing the user the deduction path carried out. Those systems which give this information are not only helping the user by explaining contradictions, but they are also expanding his knowledge.

Current applications of expert systems
An idea of the situation in France can be deduced from the proceedings of conferences such as the international meeting at Avignon (ADI 1985). The participants at Avignon received for the first time a catalogue of products, available or under development (ANL 1985). It contained a repertory of 76 products, and we know that many more exist, even if they have not yet been made known. Comparing the number of industrial products with the number of prototypes, the latter are in the majority. It is important to keep the present explosion under control.

The situation in other countries is much the same, although the emphasis may differ. A small number of industrial products and a large number of prototypes are offered to an unknown market. During previous years, the work presented was derived from academic research, particularly on theorem provers and other basic aspects. Research groups now seem to have realized that their systems need to be tested on life-sized examples, and this tendency is reflected in the style of the papers presented at Avignon. This confirms that we are at the beginning of a technology transfer process, and that expert systems are ready to be put into service.

As a survey of application fields, the list from the Avignon proceedings is indicative. We find computer aided conception, design, learning and manufacture, together with projects in architecture, robotics, mechanical conception, and electrome-chanics. On the scientific side, there is meshing, symbolic manipulation, geotechnics, geology of hydrocarburates, laser spectroscopy, chemistry, spatial geography and simulation. Real-time experiments include process control, pattern recognition (in particular voice recognition), military applications and system configuration. To this list should be added medical diagnostics, fault finding, business administration, law, financial analysis, audit and economics. And we can conclude with documentation, databases, information security, without even then being complete. Expert systems are suddenly being introduced everywhere.

It can legitimately be asked to what extent these experiments will lead to useful results. It is not for the computer specialist to judge utility in other fields; they will form their own opinions. Our role is to validate the technology, then to help other fields to apply it. It will be some years before satisfactory knowledge bases can be created for all these applications. Computing should be careful not to oversell its techniques, and should not move too quickly, in order to avoid the unfulfilled aims of the 1960s and the 1970s.

What the future holds

Together with many computer specialists and users, we are convinced that expert systems represent a significant advance in the possibilities offered by computers. While avoiding the use of words such as revolutionary or transformation of society, many new fields are being analysed, and improvements can be seen in fields already partly automated.

This positive view could lead scientists to try to go too far too fast. Artificial intelligence has regularly promised more than it was able to deliver. The phenomenon has meant that real advances have been underestimated through the rejection process provoked by the non-delivery of promised, over-ambitious products. The time is ripe for realism and common sense.

On the computing side, there already exist a large number of theorem provers. It could even be said that there are too many, since each laboratory seems to have made at least one. These provers are sufficiently powerful for the problems analysed up till now. Their weakness is in their insufficient degree of application. However, it is now just possible to find provers which are engineered, and their number is rising rapidly. Current research will introduce more complex forms of logic, which is certainly of considerable long-term interest. But the most urgent needs are to try experimental systems in real-life situations. This requiries the creation of mixed teams of experts from various fields associated with knowledge engineers from computing backgrounds. Computing laboratories tend to have too few collaborative contacts with laboratories in other fields.

Computing technology now allows the construction of numerous systems for different applications. This means that, although research is still going on, enough has been done to allow current products to become available. But we should not underestimate the work which is to be carried out by experts in the different fields.

In order that research may be applied in practice, many years of development are needed. The first need is to dispose of excellent practitioners who can put several years' effort into the construction of a system. Of course, it is just those experts who would be the most useful who are the least available, since they have a full commitment within their professions. But it must be realized that satisfaction can only come from people with high levels of competence.

The involved experts must be familiar with rule writing techniques, which is a learning process in itself, and then we must produce complete sets of rules. Afterwards, end users also need teaching in order to allow access. The need to educate large numbers of professionals from different fields, together with that of introducing the necessary infrastructure, is already time consuming. It can also be imagined that in fields such as medicine, the use of systems will lead to a deep analysis of the whole process, by the profession, in order to clarify the roles of the computer and the practitioner. All these steps are delicate operations, since errors could turn out to be expensive.

Practitioners of different disciplines will only use expert systems if they are both useful and easy to use. The human engineering involved in creating interfaces and automated help is vital to the practical success of a system. This aspect requires investment which is comparable with that of creating the knowledge base.

One of the aims of books such as this is to convince colleagues of the interest of starting collaborative programs on a proper scale, leaving them the time necessary to reach conclusions. This would avoid the overselling of artificial intelligence once again.

If we have constantly referred to the past in describing expert systems, this is not an accident. Expert systems were not created by spontaneous generation, but they are the cementation of research which started thirty years ago in computing, and much earlier in mathematics. Past experience is thus relevant and useful. One should always beware of new buzz-words which arrive without warning in computing, where the area is already saturated. Taking expert systems out of the context of computing could turn out to be an expensive mistake.

CHAPTER 6

Programming languages for artificial intelligence

The history of programming languages for artificial intelligence is already detailed. In particular, two languages have achieved general and international notoriety. LISP, invented by John McCarthy at the end of the 1950s, has been a favourite since. It is dense, with a limited number of concepts, but its applications are unlimited. It is described on page 106. Fifteen years later, Alain Colmérauer and his group invented PROLOG, which has since become a standard in the discipline. PROLOG is described on page 114.

The success of a language depends on a set of factors, such as fashion, the creator's reputation, opportunity, commercial decisions and sheer luck. Languages which succeed have much to offer, but the others are not necessarily without interest.

LISP

The publication which announced LISP was McCarthy (1960). It gives the logical basis for the language. Following implementation at MIT, programmers have used the manual (McCarthy *et al.* 1962), which is still a classic. Amongst all the thousands of publications which have followed, Weissman (1966) was the first primer. As an introduction, Siklossy (1976) can be useful. There exist also hundreds of interpreters of LISP which are used, and thousands if student exercises are counted.

The originality of LISP is its general structure. It includes program and data in a uniform syntax. The language is strictly functional, that is that there is no assignment. A LISP program is a function, which calls other functions, and so on.

In the description which follows, the original syntax has been maintained. Given the large number of dialects and implementations, the reader may find differences between this text and the syntax accepted by his system. He will need to read carefully the documentation of the particular implementation used before starting to program. Consider first the basic data elements of LISP.

LIST STRUCTURE

The basic objects of a LISP program are not typed in the usual sense. They are represented by identifiers, with the usual lexical rules. Basic objects, known as atoms, are assembled into lists. List structure is indicated by brackets, with the following recursive rules of construction:

1) The empty list is written () or NIL.
2) A list is an object.
3) An atom is an object.
4) A space is a separator.
5) A sequence of objects surrounded by brackets is a list.

Thus, with atoms A, B, C ..., the following are objects:

A is an atom.
(A) is a list.
(A B C) is a list.
() is a list, but also an atom.
(A (B (C D)) E) is a list.

What is called an object here is often referred to as a symbolic expression, or S-expression. The only object which is both a list and an atom is the empty list NIL, or ().

Lists can be used to represent the usual artificial intelligence structures, for example a tree, as shown in Figure 22.

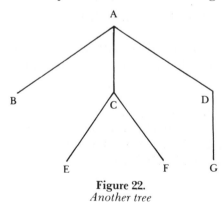

Figure 22.
Another tree

In LISP, this tree would be written:
  (A (B C (E F) D (G)))

A sub-tree appears after its parent node, in brackets.

Although trees are frequently used in artificial intelligence, they are not the only existing data structure. Lists can represent graphs in general, even if these contain loops. Recursive lists can be created, that is a list can be an element of itself.

SIMPLE OPERATIONS
Like a stack, a list can only receive new objects in its first position. The first object of a list is called its head. Taking off the head of a list leaves another list, its tail. Consider the list which led to the tree in Figure 22:

  L = (A (B C (E F) D (G)))

The head of L is A, and its tail the new list L1:

  L1 = ((B C (E F) D (G)))

The head of L1 is the list L2:

  L2 = (B C (E F) D (G))

The tail of L1 is the empty list. This results from the fact that the first object of L1 is a list. That of L was an atom.

For historical reasons, LISP uses CAR for head and CDR for tail. Suppose that the E of the list L is to be recovered. The following function would be necessary:

  CAR(CAR(CDR(CDR(CAR(CDR(L))))))

To follow this, remember that CDR (L) is L1, and CAR(L1) is L2. Thus CAR(CDR(L)) is L2, and the expression is as follows:

  CAR(CAR(CDR(CDR(L2))))
    = CAR(CAR(CDR(CDR((B C (E F) D (G))))))
    = CAR(CAR(CDR((C (E F) D (G)))))
    = CAR(CAR(((E F) D (G))))
    = CAR((E F))
    = E

To manipulate lists with these functions obviously requires training. Note that some implementations allow abbreviations to avoid brackets. For example, in the above sequence:

CAR(CAR(CDR(CAR(CDR(L))))))

can be written as:

CAADDADR(L)

CAR and CDR take apart existing lists. Their creation needs another function, CONS (for CONStruct), which has two parameters, an object and a list. The object is inserted as the head of the list. Consider some examples:

(A) = CONS(A NIL)   NIL is the empty list ()
(A B) = CONS(A CONS(B NIL))   Adds A at the front of (B)
(A (B)) = CONS(A CONS(CONS(B NIL) NIL))

The creative of the list L of the example requires the following impressive function:

L = CONS(A CONS(CONS(B CONS(C CONS(CONS(E
    CONS(F NIL))
    CONS (D CONS(CONS(G NIL) NIL))))))) NIL))

Such expressions are fortunately easier to read than they look. There is a CONS for each object. CONS(CONS(means a new level of brackets. NIL is a right bracket. This all still needs training!

In general, LISP implementations provide input/output routines which can be read and write lists in bracketed form, but attention must be taken in printing a list. One frequent error in LISP programs is printing a circular list, which tends to annoy operators as much as programmers.

SOME FUNCTIONS
ATOM tests whether its parameter is an atom. It returns T (TRUE) if it is, and NIL otherwise. For example:

ATOM(A) = T
ATOM((A)) =NIL

ATOM(()) = T   NIL is an atom and a list
ATOM((())) = NIL

EQ tests the equality of two atoms:

EQ(A A) = T
EQ(A B) = NIL
EQ((A) (A)) = NIL   (A) is not an atom

NULL tests whether its parameter is the empty list:

NULL(()) = T
NULL(NIL) = T
NULL()   illegal – no parameter
NULL(A) = NIL
NULL((A B)) = NIL
NULL((())) = NIL

the parameter is a list which has another list (empty) inside

As in other programming languages, these basic functions can be used to make new functions, defined by the programmer. The appropriate key word is DEFINE.

DEFINE, COND, LAMDA

In progressing to writing functions, note that a function is itself a list, and indeed that a LISP program is a list. As usual, we work through examples.

Suppose that L is a linear list, that is that all its objects are atoms. The function ISIN will test whether a given atom is in the list, with the following form:

(DEFINE (ISIN (procedure body)))

The function ISIN has two parameters, introduced by LAMDA:

(DEFINE (ISIN (LAMDA (AT LIST) ...)))

The term LAMDA comes from the calculus of the same name, invented by Church (1956). It describes the substitution of formal parameters by actuals. In the example, the formals AT

109

.and LIST are replaced by the corresponding actuals. The scope of LAMDA is the second pair of brackets which follow them.

The function is written recursively, using the conditional function COND. COND is followed by a series of pairs (Boolean, action), as in the following:

(COND (c1 a1)
  (c2 a2)
  ...
  (cn an))

Evaluating the COND means evaluating the first action ai for which the corresponding condition ci is TRUE. Thus, c1 is evaluated. If it is TRUE, a1 is evaluated and the COND is finished, otherwise c2 is evaluated, and so on. If no ci is TRUE, then the COND has value NIL.

Under these conditions, ISIN takes the form of Program 11.

```
(DEFINE
     (ISIN
          (LAMDA (AT LIST)
               (COND (NULL(LIST) NIL)
                     (EQ(AT CAR(LIST)) T)
                     (T ISIN(AT CDR(LIST)))
))))
```

Program 11.
ISIN

This program defines a function ISIN with two parameters AT and LIST. If the LIST is empty, the result is NIL. Otherwise, if AT is the head of LIST, the result is T. Otherwise the search is continued in the tail of LIST by a recursive call of ISIN. Since the condition T is always TRUE, it replaces the ELSE of normal programming languages. Note that the layout of the program makes it relatively easier to read. It also considerably helps the program writer, particularly in the process of counting brackets. As for BEGIN–END pairs, vertical alignment and tabulation are the crux of the method.

As a last example here, consider a frequently used function which is the concatenation of two lists. Given the lists L1 and L2, APPEND(L1 L2) makes a new list by putting L2 behind L1, and taking away the last right bracket of L1 and the first left bracket of L2. For example:

APPEND((A (B C))   ((Q R))) = (A (B C) (Q R))

APPEND can be defined as in Program 12.

```
(DEFINE
    (APPEND
        (LAMDA (L1 L2)
            (COND (NULL(L1) L2)
                (T CONS(CAR(L1) APPEND(CDR(L1) L2)))
))))
```

Program 12.
APPEND

The reader wishing to gain experience with LISP ought to go through the set of classic examples of this type.

IN THE COMPUTER

One of the advantages of LISP is the simplicity of its implementation. In general, the basic functions CAR, CDR, CONS work on boxes which represent the objects in, and the structure of, the lists in the program. Consider the previous example:

(A (B C (E F) D (G)))

Creation starts with the right-most object. Each call of CONS takes a new box with two entries, the left hand one for the CAR and the right hand one for the CDR. CONS(G NIL) forces the initialization of the box in Figure 23.

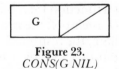

Figure 23.
CONS(G NIL)

Call this list L1. CONS(L1 NIL), that is ((G)), is now produced, as in Figure 24.

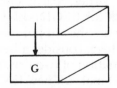

Figure 24.
CONS(CONS(G NIL) NIL)

111

Continuing in the same manner, the complete list in Figure 25 is produced.

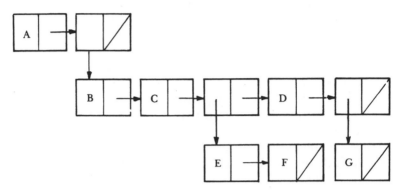

Figure 25.
Representation by pointers

	CAR	CDR
1	A	2
2	3	-1
3	B	4
4	C	5
5	6	7
6	E	8
7	D	9
8	F	-1
9	10	-1
10	G	-1

Figure 26.
Representation of a list as an array

Obviously, in practice, the boxes are kept in an array with two entries per element. List structure can be represented on two vectors, one called CAR and the other CDR. A pointer is the index of the vector entry referenced. For this list, the array in Figure 26 could be obtained, with NIL represented by –1.

The array looks like the one used to represent a binary tree (Figure 4, Chapter 2), and the structure is, in fact, the same. As it happens, it is this structure which was historically responsible for the use of CAR and CDR. In the first implementation, on the IBM machine of the time, and two elements CAR and CDR were stored in half-words, and the machine instructions which referenced half-words were called CAR and CDR.

IMPLEMENTATIONS

A LISP program is a list. It is executed by submission to an interpreter. The tradition is that the interpreter is itself written in LISP. This encourages implementers to use the same version of the language, in order to assure program portability. Note that this result has not been obtained in practice.

Many of the dialects which have been invented contain noticeable differences compared with the original LISP. Amongst these there are:

1) Dot notation. The list (A B C) becomes (A.B.C.NIL). With this notation, some interpreters accept lists with an atom as CDR, for example (A.B.C).
2) The use of the quote symbol to indicate evaluation of an object.
3) Efforts towards either structuring LISP by adding traditional syntactic forms, such as IF THEN ELSE, to make programs more readable, or incorporating LISP structures into standard languages such as the ALGOL family. The results have shocked purists, but have helped programmers in writing programs such as compilers.

PRACTICALITIES

All the data structures needed in artificial intelligence programs can be represented in LISP. This is one of the reasons why the language is used in this context. Only a psychologist can say whether LISP corresponds to a 'natural' approach or not, but it has certainly fascinated its users. To illustrate a small use in one application, consider again a problem already used as an example.

In the couples problem presented on page 49, if A is found to be married to a known man, the other three men are eliminated from her list of possible husbands. The elimination function could take the form of Program 13, where L1, an atom, is eliminated from the list L2.

```
(DEFINE
  (ELIM
    (LAMDA (L1 L2)
      (COND
        (NULL(L2) NIL)
        (EQ(L1 CAR(L2)) CDR(L2))
        (T CONS(CAR(L2) ELIM(L1 CDR(L2))))
))))
```

Program 13.
ELIM

An application program is made up of a set of functions of this type, which call each other, usually recursively.

PROLOG

Created by Alain Colmérauer and his group in the early 1970s, PROLOG, because of its formal style, has been considered a successor to LISP. However, it is certainly not an extension of LISP, since the formal base is different. LISP uses lamda calculus, whereas PROLOG uses predicate calculus. It is perhaps because of its originality that PROLOG has needed time to become established, even though it was known to specialists from the start.

Over the last few years, PROLOG has become very popular, and systems have been implemented on a wide range of computers. Like LISP, PROLOG has risen from a specialized language to assume international status. A big push for the language was the Japanese decision to base their fifth generation computers on artificial intelligence, with PROLOG as the basic tool. It is as yet too early to evaluate completely the effects of this decision.

Whatever final evaluation is made of PROLOG, it needs to be learnt to penetrate the world of artificial intelligence. The language is particularly appreciated for teaching, research and the experimentation of new systems. Whether industrial applications will be programmed on a large scale in PROLOG is at the moment unknown, and to a certain extent not important.

In a general text, it is not possible to cover all the aspects of PROLOG, the more so since, like LISP, It has already several dialects. The examples given here are written in the current Marseille version, PROLOG II. As Anglosaxon variants are widely distributed, with different syntax, prospective users will once again need to consult their own documentation. In this book, it is simply hoped to give readers a taste of what PROLOG is like in order to form their own judgement.

BASIC ELEMENTS

A PROLOG program is a set of facts and rules which describe a universe. It works on named objects. A fact is represented by a predicate followed by a right pointing arrow and a semi-colon. For example, taking (once again!) the couples problem presented on page 49, the following facts can be expressed:

```
woman(ann) -> ;
woman(beatrice) -> ;
woman(charlotte) -> ;
woman(danielle) -> ;
man(eric) -> ;
man(frank) -> ;
man(george) -> ;
man(humphrey) -> ;
```

A fact F -> ; reads F is true in the described universe. Object names are identifiers which start with at least two letters.

Questions can be asked about facts. A question does not contain the assertive arrow. As PROLOG is conversational, the system replies by yes or no, unfortunately indicated by a new line or now new line, as in the following examples:

```
woman(ann);
woman(martine);    – martine is unknown
man(george);
woman(george);
```

Yes means that the system confirms the hypothesis, no that either it has found a contradiction, or that the fact is unknown.

PROLOG also has variables, which are written as identifiers made up of one letter, followed optionally by a number of figures. Variables are often used to establish definitions by relations between objects, called rules. Rules are the deductions that can be drawn in the considered universe. They contain variables which are the same as those of logic. Consider the following rule:

A(x) -> B(x);

This reads A(x) is TRUE, if B(x) is TRUE. A PROLOG rule can be considered to be an implication, where the direction of the arrow is in the opposite sense of that usually used. For example, consider the following rules about marriage:

married(x,) -> woman(x) man(y);

Although the given facts are true, since marriages are between a woman and a man, the definition is not sufficient. In fact, it says that each existing woman is married to each man. Definitions must be complete. Another relation, this time correct, could be:

brothers(x,y) -> man(x) man(y) father(x,a) father(y,a)
              mother(x,b) mother(y,b) dif(x,y);

Under these conditions, x and y are effectively brothers. Note the necessity to indicate, by dif(x,y), that they represent two different people, since otherwise each man would be his own brother. The conditions after the arrow are verified one after the other, and are logically connected by an implicit AND.

Suppose now that we wish to introduce the notion of half brothers, that is men with either the same father or the same mother. This takes two rules, linked by an implicit OR:

half-brothers(x,y) -> man(x) man(y) dif(x,y)
                   father(x,a) father(y,a);
half-brothers(x,y) -> man(x) man(y) dif(x,y)
                   mother(x,a) mother(y,a);

x and y are half brothers if the first rule is verified, or if the second is verified. With these definitions, brothers are also half brothers. This could have been avoided by another use of dif in each rule. Note that the same identifier, a, occurs in both rules, but stands for different objects. The scope of a variable is the rule in which it occurs.

This method of combining AND and OR follows the standard clausal form, PROLOG being built on Horn clauses.

IMPLEMENTATION

One of the basic principles of PROLOG interpreters is backtracking, as studied in Chapter 3. Consider the (doubtful) definition of marriage given in the previous section. The system has a list of facts which says who are the four men and who the four women. Take the following question:

married(x,y);

The interpreter looks for pairs (x,y) which satisfy the given definition:

married(x,y) -> woman(x) man(y);

It examines the clauses in the order in which they occur in the program, which means finding first the name of a woman. Since ann is the first such name, ann is associated with x, and this information is stacked. In normal computing one could say ann is assigned to x, but PROLOG says x is instantiated by ann. With the first instantiation on the stack, the interpreter tries to satisfy the second, and last, clause man(y). As eric is the first man's name, it prints:

x=ann   y=eric

Having found one solution, the interpreter will now look for others by backtracking on the stack. The last decision, on top of the stack, is the instantiation of y by eric. The system will look for more men's names, printing successively:

x=ann   y=frank
x=ann   y=george
x=ann   y=humphrey

This time there are no men's names left, so backtracking goes down to the previous decision, which instantiated x with ann. The next woman's name is beatrice, and the process starts again. The interpreter will repeat the complete list of men's names for each woman, in the same way as the examples in

117

Chapter 3 started again after going down the stack. The interpreter will finish the list of all possible couples:

    x=beatrice   y=eric
    x=beatrice   y=frank
    x=beatrice   y=george
    x=beatrice   y=humphrey
    x=charlotte y=eric
    x=charlotte y=frank
    x=charlotte y=george
    x=charlotte y=humphrey
    x=danielle   y=eric
    x=danielle   y=frank
    x=danielle   y=george
    x=danielle   y=humphrey

On such a simple example, backtracking can look trivial. In fact, the technique is quite powerful, since it allows automatic testing of all hypotheses. As in the example given in Chapter 3, the interpreter looks for solutions over the whole possibility tree, trying to instantiate each variable with each object, in classic depth first search order.

DATA STRUCTURES

It has been said that PROLOG is not a LISP variant, but for obvious reasons, it also contains list structures. Their treatment is an example of the differences between the two languages.

A PROLOG list has the same structure as a LISP one, except that PROLOG usually used the dot notation. The example list given on page 106 is written in LISP as follows:

(A (B (C D)) E)

In PROLOG we could write:

(s.(b.(c.d.nil).nil).e.nil)

In this style, the dot stands for an application of CONS in LISP. Each true list starts by applying CONS with the empty list NIL as second parameter. This explains the occurrences of nil before each right bracket. PROLOG allows lists which do not end with NIL. In fact, in PROLOG, nil is not a predefined predicate, but a constant that could be any two or more letter identifier. It indicates the end of an instantiation because a constant cannot be instantiated.

In order to show up style differences between LISP and PROLOG, consider the PROLOG rules which decide whether a given atom is contained in a given linear list. The rules for member (x,y) look to see if x is a member of the linear list y.

    member(x,x.z) -> ;
    member(x,z.y) -> ;

The first rule says that if the looked for object x is the head of the list y, then x is a member of y. The second rule says that if x is not the head of the list, then it is a member of the list if it is a member of the tail of the list. The programming technique resembles that of LISP, but it is no longer necessary to take into account the cases of failure, since these are eliminated by the backtracking mechanism.

Conceptually, the most important data structure in PROLOG is once again the tree, in a sense somewhat larger than the strict mathematical definition previously given. Lists are representations of trees. The equivalence of two trees may require instantiations in order to allow unification, as shown on page 74. The two trees must first have the same structure. Then substitutions are envisaged, which lead to instantiations. For example, consider the two trees in Figure 27, which represent arithmetic expressions.

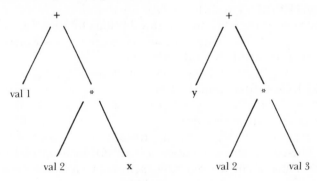

Figure 27.
Unification of two trees

In Figure 27, val1, val2, val3 are values, and x and y variables. It is intuitively obvious that, in order to make the two trees equal, x must be instantiated by val3, and y by val1. The two occurrences of val2 are coherent, which is fortunate, since otherwise unification could not take place. Consider now the case where the occurrences of val2 are replaced by variables p and q as in Figure 28.

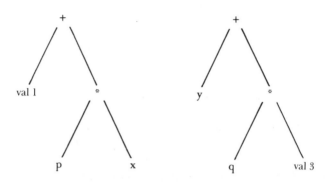

Figure 28.
More unification

This time x and y are instantiated, but p and q are not. Nevertheless, p and q must be instantiated to the same object. They must, therefore, be linked, so that instantiation of the one will lead to instantiation of the other.

On simple examples like these, unification looks easy. It becomes more difficult when the trees are infinite.

ADDITIONAL FEATURES

The preceding sections give a false idea of PROLOG in the sense that the language is much wider than is indicated. Many other possibilities are offered.

Although PROLOG was not designed with numerical calculation in mind, it contains the necessary minimum. Integers and real numbers are recognized objects, as are the usual arithmetic operators. Expressions are formally trees of the type seen above. Note that instantiation does not provoke the evaluation of expressions. The PROLOG equivalent of an arithmetic assignment is the function val, as in the following:

val(add(7.1).x)

This provokes the evaluation of the expression add(7,1), x being instantiated to the value 8 which results.

In each implementation of PROLOG, there is also a set of communication functions, that is input-output and an operating system interface. They are not discussed here, since they have little effect on the principles of the language. The PROLOG user will, in any case, be forced to consult his detailed, local documentation.

A PARTIAL SYNTHESIS

PROLOG started slowly, since its creators did not invest heavily in publications or sales, and its originality means that it was assimilated slowly. Its present success is all the more worthy of merit that it results from its intrinsic qualities. The Japanese decision to adopt PROLOG for the fifth generation product raised it to international status. Everything indicates that it is time to try and evaluate its place in the applications considered here.

PROLOG is used currently in research and teaching, in a wide sense. In development it also allows new ideas to be tested, and to get used to patterns of thinking useful in problem solving. A generation of academic computer specialists strongly influenced by its style are now leaving university. The future effect will be considerable.

It remains to be seen whether the product can become industrial. Our opinion, not necessarily shared by all our colleagues, is that much work remains to be done on the language before it can be put into everyday use. Up to now, it has been the dialects of PROLOG which took into account keyboard differences, or national character sets. This was followed by an increase in the power of the language with PROLOG II. We now need some stabilization, which will absorb the strong points of PROLOG, while adding properties which will allow its distribution to a wider audience. Problems like readability, the lack of redundancy, the use of lexical gadgets to distinguish, for example, variables from objects all have to be faced. Although some claims have been made in the direction of friendliness, the final job still needs doing. The arrival on the market of friendly versions of PROLOG, in industrial implementations, will allow users to gain all the benefits from the ideas that PROLOG can offer.

121

Exercises

Programming exercises in LISP or PROLOG are readily available.

IN LISP

1) Write a procedure to inverse the order of a list, that is that takes a list as input, and outputs the same list with the objects in reverse order.
2) Write the above inverse procedure, inverting also all the sublists of the list.
3) Write an atomize procedure, which takes in a structured list and outputs the same list without structure, that is a linear list containing the atoms inside the list and its sublists. The atoms must be in the same order in the linear list as in the original.
4) Examine the effect of running the preceding programs on circular (recursive) lists.

IN PROLOG

1) Redo in **PROLOG** the **LISP** problems.
2) Suppose there exists a set of relations concerning families including father(x,y) and mother(x,y); mother(x,y) says that y is the mother of x. Write a rule to find first cousins.
3) Create a family, as above, and foresee the effects of a call of brothers(x,y) from page 117. The aim is to confirm the reader's understanding of the backtrack process, that is the order of instantiation in the interpreter.
4) Translate the problem given on page 78 directly into **PROLOG**.
5) Write the programs, such as the labyrinth or the couples problems, in **PROLOG**. The job requires a certain mastery of the language.

CHAPTER 7
Conclusion

After structured programming, software engineering and many others, artificial intelligence has become the current popular buzz-word in computing. As usual, new groups of specialists have come to the surface, many of which are technically competent. Current or prospective computer users are naturally led to communicate with such groups in order to examine possibilities of applying artificial intelligence in their context. While strongly encouraging this trend, we wish to put the development in its context in order to avoid, or at least to diminish, the numerous painful experiences that can result from a naive and over-trusting approach.

Artificial intelligence is a part of computing. This statement leads to two less obvious conclusions. First, those who imply that a new revolution is under way, and that traditional computing is out of date and unnecessary, are dishonest, naive or incompetent. They should be avoided. Second, artificial intelligence products should be judged in the same way as other computing products. Since we consider the field as being an evolution within a discipline, all the usual questions should be asked, and tests carried out, before installing a new system simply because the title is fashionable. Legitimate and necessary questions to be put include: 'What needs are answered?', 'How much does it cost?', 'What training is necessary for the operators and users?', 'Who can we consult who already uses the system?'.

Expert systems, and other products using artificial intelligence, are ready for installation and use in practical applications. Since field testing is not yet complete, we need to get over the step of practical experimentation on a moderate scale, with conscious and intelligent users. Large-scale installation will take place over the next few years. Prospective users must have realistic aims and be ready to invest in this future.

This book is an attempt towards the understanding of artificial intelligence by non-specialists. It can be used by professionals from different fields, by students, or by computer specialists who are looking for an introduction. Understanding a subject is only a first step. We do not pretend that readers will be able to write their own systems, but we hope that they will choose their products on a more rational basis.

Any subject which receives as much publicity as this one must give rise to numerous books and papers. Interesting surveys (the list is short and very incomplete) are Scown (1985) and Wos *et al.* (1984). Further study will necessarily lead to writing programs in specialized languages such as PROLOG, using manuals such as Giannesini *et al.* (1985).

Artificial intelligence will have come of age when the term becomes unnecessary. At that moment in time, the techniques discussed here will be common place, and will not need a generic, and vague, term to describe them. Given the usual rate of evolution in computing, this will take about ten or fifteen years to come about. An interesting field of speculation is to predict the buzz-word of the last decade of this century – we are content to leave such speculation to our readers.

References

ADI *5èmes journées internationales, les systèmes experts et leurs applications* Agence pour l'informatique, Avignon, May 1985.

AFCET *Actes troisième congrès reconnaissance de formes et intelligence artificielle* Nancy, September 1981.

AFCET *Actes quatrième congrès reconnaissance des formes et intelligence artificielle* Paris, January 1984.

ANL *Catalogue des prototypes de recherche en logiciel, extrait intelligence artificielle/systèmes experts* Association nationale de logiciel, special edition given with (ADI 1985).

Asimov, I. *The Robots* 1950, reprinted in *The Complete Robot* Granada, 1983.

Barron, D.W. *Recursive Techniques in Programming* Macdonald Computer Monographs, 1968.

Bauer, F.L.; Samelson, K. (eds) *Language Hierarchies and Interfaces* Springer Verlag, 1976.

Bauer, F.L.; Broy, M. (eds) *Program Construction* Springer Verlag, 1979.

Baumann, R.H.; Licklide, J.C.R. An electronic word recognizer, *Journal of the Acoustical Society of America* **26**, 137, 1954.

Berge, C. *The Theory of Graphs and its Applications* Methuen, 1962.

Bobrow, D.G.; Kaplan, R.M.; Kay, M.; Norman. D.A.; Thompson, H.; Winograd, T. GUS, A frame driven dialogue system, *Artificial Intelligence* **8,2**, pp. 155–173, 1977.

Bolc, L. *Representation and Processing of Natural Language* Hanser, 1980.

Bourelly, L.; Hesnault, A. Presentation at the *Congress of Artificial Intelligence* Avignon, May 1984.

Burstall, R. M.; Darlington, J. Some transformations for

developing recursive programs, *SIGPLAN Notices* June 1975.

Chang, C.L.; Lee, R.C. *Symbolic Logic and Mechanical Theorem Proving* Academic Press, 1979.

Chomsky, N. *Aspects of the Theory of Syntax* MIT Press, 1965.

Chouraqui, E. Contribution à l'étude théorique de la représentation de connaissance, *Le système symbolique ARCHES* Thesis, Nancy, 1981.

Church, A. An unsolvable problem of number theory, *American Journal of Mathematics* 58, pp. 345–363, 1936.

Church, A. *Introduction to Mathematical Logic* Princeton University Press, 1956.

Clarke, M.R.B. (ed.) *Advances in Computer Chess 1* Edinburgh University Press, 1977.

Clarke, M.R.B. (ed.) *Advances in Computer Chess 2* Edinburgh University Press, 1980.

Collins, N.L.; Michie, D. (eds) *Machine Intelligence 1* Oliver and Boyd, Edinburgh, 1967.

Colmérauer, A; Kanoui, H.; Paséro, R.; Roussel, Ph. *Un système de communication homme-machine en français* GIA Marseille, 1973.

Colmérauer, A. Private communication, 1981.

Colmérauer, A. *PROLOG II, manuel de référence et modèle théorique* GIA Marseille, 1982.

Davis, K.H.; Biddulph, R; Balashek, S. Automatic recognition of spoken digits in (Jackson 1953).

Davis, M. A computer program for Pressburger's procedure *Summer Institute for Symbolic Logic* 1957, reprinted in (Siekman 1983).

Davis, M. The prehistory and early history of automated deduction in (Siekman 1983).

Davis, M.; Putnam, H. A computing procedure for quantification theory, *JACM* **7**, July 1960.

Duda, R.O.; Hart, P.E.; Konolige, K.; Reboh, R., *A Computer Based Consultant for Mineral Exploration* Technical report, SRI International, September 1979.

Elcock, E.W.; Murray, A.M. Experiments with a learning component in a GO-MOKU playing program in (Collins 1967).

Feigenbaum, E.A.; Feldman, J. (eds) *Computers and Thought* McGraw-Hill, 1963.

Friedberg, R.M. Learning machines, parts 1 & 2, *IBM Journal of Research & Development* **2 & 3**, pp. 2–13 and 282–287, 1958, 1959.

Fry, D.B.; Denis, P. Experiments in mechanical speech recognition in (Jackson 1953).

Gerard, M.; Mercier, G. L'apprentissage des paramètres de reconnaissance phonétique dans un système de reconnaissance de la parole continue in (AFCET 1981).

Giannesini, F.; Kanoui, H.; Pasero, R.; van Caneghem, M. *Prolog* InterEditions, 1985.

Griffiths, M. Program production by successive transformation in (Bauer 1976).

Griffiths, M. Development of the Schorr-Waite algorithm in (Bauer 1979).

Hayes, J.E.; Michie, D.; Mikulich, L.I. (eds), *Machine Intelligence 9* Ellis Horwood, 1979.

Herbrand, J. Recherches sur la théorie de la démonstration, *Trav. soc. sci. et lettres* Warsaw CL3 1930.

Hoare, C.A.R.; Wirth, N. *An Axiomatic Definition of the Programming Language PASCAL* CS report no. 6, Zurich, November 1972.

Huxley, A. *Brave New World* 1932, reprinted by Chatto and Windus, 1984.

IEEE, *IEEE Proceedings, International Conferences on Pattern Recognition* (seven such conferences up to now in an ongoing regular series which started 15 years ago).

Jackson, W. (ed.) *Proceedings of the Second London Symposium on Applications of Communications Theory* Butterworth, 1953.

J&S, Le bureau, *Jeux et Stratégie* **25**, p. 62, February–March 1984a.

J&S, Qui est mécanicien?, *Jeux et Stratégie* **26**, p. 84, April–May 1984b.

Kent, A. (ed.) *Information Retrieval and Mechanical Translation* (2 vols), Interscience Publishers, 1961.

Knuth, D.E. *The Art of Computer Programming, vol. 1, Fundamental Algorithms* Addison-Wesley, 1968.

Kowalski, R.A. *Logic for Problem Solving, Artificial Intelligence series* North-Holland, 1979.

Latombe, J.C. (ed.) *Artificial Intelligence and Pattern Recognition in Computer Aided Design* North-Holland, 1978.

Laurière, J.L. *Représentation et utilisation de connaissances: les systèmes experts, TSI 1, nos. 1 and 2* 1982.

Levy, D. *Techniques de programmation des jeux* Editions du PSI, 1983.

Loveland, D.W. *Automated Theorem Proving: A Logical*

Basis North-Holland, 1978.

McCarthy, J.T. *Programs with Common Sense* Stanford, 1958, reprinted in (Minsky 1968).

McCarthy, J.T. Recursive functions of symbolic expressions and their computation by machine, part 1, *CACM* **3,4**, pp. 185-195, April 1960.

McCarthy, J.T.; Abrahams, P.W.; Edwards, D.J.; Hart, T.P.; Levin, M.I.; *LISP 1.5 Programmer's Manual* MIT Press, 1962.

McCarthy, J.T. History of LISP, *ACM SIGPLAN notices* **13,8**, pp. 217-223, August 1978.

McDermott, J. R1: A rule based configurer of computer systems, *Artificial Intelligence* **19**, pp. 39-88, September 1982.

Marsland, T.A. A bibliography of computer chess in (Hayes 1979).

Meissenberg, E. Schach liche leistungen von computer, *Deutsche Schachblatter* pp. 1-4, 1968.

Michie, D. Mathematical games, *Scientific American* March 1962.

Michie, D. (ed.) *Machine Intelligence 3* Edinburgh University Press, 1968.

Michie, D.; Fleming, J.G.; Oldfield, J.V. A comparison of heuristic, interactive and unaided methods of solving a shortest route problem in (Michie 1968).

Minsky, M. (ed.) *Semantic Information Processing* MIT Press, 1968.

Minsky, M. A framework for representing knowledge in (Winston 1975).

Mittman, B. First world computer chess championship at IFIP Congress, Stockholm, *CACM* **17**, p. 604, 1974.

Newborn, M.M. A review of the first and second US computer championships and an analysis of recent developments in computer chess, *ACM72 Computer chess notes* pp. 1-9, 1972.

Newell, A.; Shaw, J.C.; Simon, H. Empirical explorations with the logical theory machine, *Proceedings of WJCC* 1957, reprinted in (Siekman 1983).

Orwell, G. *1984* Warburg, 1949.

Richter, H. The first German computer chess championship at Dortmund, *SIGART Newsletter* **56**, p. 2, 1976.

Robinson, J.A. A machine-orientated logic based on the resolution principle, *JACM* **12**, January 1965.

Robinson, J.A. *Logic: Form and Function* Edinburgh University Press and Elsevier North-Holland, 1979.

Rosenberg, R.S. Approaching discourse computationally: a review in (Bolc 1980).

Roussel, Ph. *PROLOG: manuel de référence et utilisation* GIA Marseille, 1975.

Salkoff, M. *Une grammaire en chaîne du français* Dunod, 1973.

Samuels, A.L. Some studies in machine learning using the game of checkers, *IBM Journal of Research and Development* 3, pp. 210-229, 1959, reprinted in (Faigenbaum 1963).

Schorr, H.; Waite, W.M. An efficient machine independent procedure for garbage collection in various list structures, *CACM* August 1967.

Shannon, C.E. Programming a computer for playing chess, *Philosophical Magazine* 7, pp. 256-275, 1950.

Shortliffe, E. *Computer Based Consultation: MYCIN* Elsevier, 1976.

Siekman, J.; Wrightson, G. (eds) *Automation of Reasoning 1* Springer Verlag, 1983.

Siklossy, L. *Let's Talk LISP* Prentice-Hall, 1976.

Souls, S; Marsland, T.A. Canadian computer chess tournament, *SIGART Newsletter* 54, pp. 12-13, 1975.

Turing, A.M. On computable numbers, with an application to the Entscheidungsproblem, *Proceedings of the London Mathematical Society* 42, pp. 230-264, 1936.

Turing, A.M. Computing machinery and intelligence, *Mind* 59, pp. 433-460, 1950.

Warshall, S. A theorem on Boolean matrices, *JACM* 9, 1, January 1962.

Weissman, C. *LISP 1.5 Primer* Dickenson, 1966.

Weizenbaum, J. ELIZA - A computer program for the study of natural language communication between man and machine, *CACM* 9,1, pp. 36-45, 1966.

Whitehead, A.; Russell, B. *Principia Mathematica* Cambridge University Press, 1910.

Winston, P.H. (ed.) *The Psychology of Computer Vision* McGraw-Hill, 1975.

Wos, L.; Overbeek, R.; Lusk, E.; Boyle, J. *Automated Reasoning* Prentice-Hall, 1984.

Yngve, V. MT at the MIT, *Proceedings of the Symposium on Machine Translation* Prentice-Hall, 1961.

Zuse, K. *Plankalkul* 1945, reprinted in report no. 106, GMD Bonn, 1976.

The algorithmic language used

For many of the programs given in this book, the language is rather like PASCAL, with a few small changes. Some of these are as follows.

Comments start with -- and carry on to the end of the line (as in ADA). The semi-colon is a separator and not a terminator. Keywords are in capital letters, identifiers in lower case.

Expressions. They are written as in PASCAL, but with the additional operators CAND and COR. x CAND y is FALSE if x is false, y not being evaluated in this case. If x is TRUE, then the value of x CAND y is y. Similarly, x COR y is TRUE if x is true, y not being evaluated, and takes the value of y if x is FALSE. These operators allow testing of a first condition, for example if an index is within the bounds of an array, before evaluating the second part, which may for example contain an array reference. CASE may also be used to deliver an expression.

Assignment statements may take two forms:
    Variable: = Expression
or (List of variables): = Procedure call

The variables in the list are of the types given by the RETURN statement of the procedure.

Loops can be of two forms, and are completely bracketed to avoid writing large numbers of BEGIN–END pairs:

    WHILE Condition
    DO Statements
    DONE
or FOR List
    DO Statements
    DONE

The list after FOR has the usual form.

Conditions are also always completely bracketed, with or without an ELSE part:

IF Condition
THEN Statements
ELSE Statements
FI

or   IF Condition
THEN Statements
FI

Procedure declarations can return zero or more values, and have the form:

PROCEDURE Name(Parameters) RETURNS (Types);
Body ENDPROC;

If the procedure does not return a value, the RETURNS part is absent. If the procedure returns just one value, its type can follow RETURNS without brackets. Parameters are as in PASCAL, but some programs are given without complete specifications.

The RETURN statement indicates the value, or values, which are the result of the procedure call. It has the form:

RETURN (List of values)

The values in the list have the same types as those given in the RETURNS statement. When only one result is returned, the brackets can be left out. When only one result is returned, the brackets can be left out. A procedure with no result can contain RETURN without a following value.

Other declarations follow PASCAL. When the declaration is obvious, it is often omitted.

APPENDIX 2
Solutions to certain exercises

The solutions to most of the exercises which are programs are given here. In other cases, solutions are open, or the questions were put to stimulate reflection. These are left to the reader. Programs are usually written in the algorithmic language used in the text. They will need some small amount of rewriting to run with a particular compiler on a particular machine.

Solutions to exercises on page 37

```
1a) PROCEDURE findname(node,person) RETURNS bool;
        found:=name(node)=person;
        IF NOT found AND exists(lfoll(node))
        THEN found:=findname(lfoll(node),person)
        FI;
        IF NOT found AND exists(rfoll(node))
        THEN found:=findname(rfoll(node),person)
        FI;
        RETURN found
    ENDPROC;
    findname(adam,"jean")
-- adam is the node whose name is "adam"

1b)  PROCEDURE grandf(node,old,young) RETURNS bool;
        found:=FALSE;
        IF name(node)=old
        THEN found:=name(lfoll(lfoll(node)))=young OR
                    name(rfoll(lfoll(node)))=young OR
                    name(lfoll(rfoll(node)))=young OR
                    name(rfoll(rfoll(node)))=young
        FI;
    -- These tests assume that non existent followers point to a
    -- fictional  node which is its own left and right  follower
    -- and which has a new name.
        IF NOT found AND exists(lfoll(node))
        THEN found:=grandf(lfoll(node),old,young)
        FI;
        IF NOT found AND exists(rfoll(node))
        THEN found:=grandf(rfoll(node),old,young)
        FI;
        RETURN found
    ENDPROC;
    grandf(adam,"matthew","john")
```

133

```
lc)   PROCEDURE cousin(node,a,b) RETURN bool;
         found:=((name(lfoll(lfoll(node)))=a OR
                  name(rfoll(lfoll(node)))=a) AND
                 (name(lfoll(rfoll(node)))=b OR
                  name(rfoll(rfoll(node)))=b)) OR
                ((name(lfoll(lfoll(node)))=b OR
                  name(rfoll(lfoll(node)))=b) AND
                 (name(lfoll(rfoll(node)))=a OR
                  name(rfoll(rfoll(node)))=a));
      -- with  the   same  suppositions  concerning   inexistent
      -- followers as in the previous example.
         IF NOT found AND exists(lfoll(node))
         THEN found:=cousin(lfoll(node,a,b)
         FI;
         IF NOT found AND exists(rfoll(node))
         THEN found:=cousin(rfoll(node),a,b)
         FI;
         RETURN found
      ENDPROC;
      cousin(adam,"john","jean")
```

2) Take the transitive closure of the matrix. If the result is a matrix which is all ones, the original is connex, otherwise it will break up into a set of sub-matrices, each of which is full, which correspond to the independent subgraphs.

3) All the nodes accessible from the root figure as ones in the line of the transitive closure matrix which corresponds to the root.

Solutions to exercises on page 61

1) Compared to the mouse, the cheese is in a given quarter of the world, in general between two possible directions. The procedure finds the preferred direction from (x,y) towards (xc,yc).

```
PROCEDURE prefdir(x,y,xc,yc) RETURNS integer;
   RETURN IF yc>=y          -- northern half
       THEN IF xc<x         -- western quarter
           THEN 4
           ELSE IF yc=y
               THEN 2
               ELSE 1
               FI
           FI
       ELSE IF xc>x         -- eastern quarter, south
           THEN 2
           ELSE 3
           FI
       FI
ENDPROC;
```

```
BEGIN barrier: ARRAY (1..8,1..8,1..4) OF bool;
      mark: ARRAY (1..8,1..8) OF bool;
      pile: ARRAY (1..65) OF integer;
      x,y,xn,yn,xm,ym,xc,yc: integer;
      dir: integer;
      x:=xm; y:=ym; mark(x,y):=TRUE; dir:=0; push(0);
      WHILE NOT(x=xc AND y=yc)
      DO IF NOT(dir=pred(prefdir(x,y,xc,yc)))
-- pred  is the direction preceeding its parameter (dir-1  unless
-- dir=1, when pred=4)
         THEN IF dir=0
                 THEN dir:=prefdir(x,y,xc,yc)
                 ELSE dir:=dir+1;
                      IF dir>4
                      THEN dir:=1
                      FI
              FI;
              xn:= CASE dir OF (x,x+1,x,x-1) ESAC;
              yn:= CASE dir OF (y+1,y,y-1,y) ESAC;
              IF NOT barrier(x,y,dir) CAND NOT mark(xn,yn)
              THEN x:=xn; y:=yn; mark(x,y):=TRUE;
                      push(dir); dir:=0
              FI
         ELSE pull(dir);
              IF dir=0
              THEN -- no solution exists
              FI;
              CASE dir
              OF 1: y:=y-1,
                 2: x:=x-1,
                 3: y:=y+1,
                 4: x:=x+1
              ESAC
         FI
      DONE
   END

2.
BEGIN PROCEDURE path(x,y:integer) RETURNS bool;
         IF x=xf AND y=yf
         THEN RETURN TRUE
         ELSE dir:=0; found:=FALSE;
              WHILE dir<4 AND NOT found
              DO dir:=dir+1;
                 xn:=CASE dir OF (x,x+1,x,x-1) ESAC;
                 yn:=CASE dir OF (y+1,y,y-1,y) ESAC;
                 IF NOT barrier(x,y,dir) CAND NOT mark(xn,yn)
                 THEN found:=path(xn,yn)
                 FI
              DONE;
              RETURN found
         FI;
      ENDPROC path;
      print(path(xm,ym))
-- will  write TRUE or FALSE following the existence or not of  a
-- path from the mouse to the cheese
END
```

135

3) Left to the reader, who should try them on his computer.
4) The program uses a chessboard which is an ARRAY of 8*8 squares. It will write in each square the minimum number of steps separating the square from the mouse. Thus, the mouse is 0 steps from itself. Direct neighbours are 1 step from the mouse, their neighbours 2, and so on, taking into account barriers and already numbered squares. The program stops at the cheese, at the same time as it discovers the length of the minimum path.

```
BEGIN barrier: ARRAY (1..8,1..8,1..4) OF bool;
    square: ARRAY (1..8,1..8) OF integer;
    x,y,xn,yn,xm,ym,xc,yc: integer;
    dist, dir: integer;
    finished: bool;
-- The ARRAY square must be initialised to -1
    square(xm,ym):=0; dist:=0; finished:=FALSE;
    WHILE NOT finished
    DO x:=1; y:=1;
-- look for squares containing the value dist so as to put dist+1
-- in neighbouring squares, starting with (1,1)
        WHILE y<9 AND NOT finished

        DO IF square(x,y)=dist
-- one has been found, so examine the four directions
            THEN dir:=0;
                WHILE dir<4 AND NOT finished
                DO dir:=dir+1;
                    IF NOT barrier(x,y,dir)
                    THEN xn:=CASE dir OF (x,x+1,x,x-1) ESAC;
                        yn:=CASE dir OF (y+1,y,y-1,y) ESAC;
                        finished:= xn=xc AND yn=yc;
                        IF NOT finished
                        THEN IF square(xn,yn)=-1
-- the square must not be already marked
                            THEN square(xn,yn):=dist+1
                            FI
                        FI
                    FI
                DONE
        FI;
        IF x=8
        THEN x:=1; y:=y+1
        ELSE x:=x+1
-- the next square
        FI
    DONE;
    dist:=dist+1
-- the next distance
    DONE
END
```

The program is not very efficient, and would be worse in an extended labyrinth. Instead of looking at every square on each round, it would be better to remember the coordinates of the squares of a given distance in a list. The list is examined each time round, and replaced by the new list for the next distance.

5) The six possible conversations are, taking into account the first constraint B talks to E:

Talks to						
	1	2	3	4	5	6
A	F	F	G	G	H	H
B	E	E	E	E	E	E
C	G	H	F	H	F	G
D	H	G	H	F	G	F

```
Case 1. F m C
        G m A
        H m A
Eliminated because A cannot be married to G and H.

Case 2. F m C
        A m G
        A m G
        D m E
Coherent. It is C who is talking with H. The other cases are
treated similarly, leaving C t H as the only possible solution.
```

6) We would be delighted to receive solutions to this non-trivial problem.

7) The procedure plays a move in position pos for the player (O or X) called who. It returns two results, the square (place) which is to be played, and the theoretical projection (win, lose or draw) in res.

```
PROCEDURE move(who,pos,place,res);
        IF finished(pos)          -- finished says that the squares
                                  -- are all full
        THEN res:=draw; place:=0;
        ELSE i:=0; win:=FALSE; drawnmove:=0;
-- i is the number of squares already tried, win is TRUE if the
-- position is a win, drawnmove is a move which leads to a
-- theoretical draw
             WHILE NOT win AND i<9
             DO i:=i+1;
                  IF pos(i)=0
                  THEN IF line(who,pos,i)
-- line is TRUE if playing in square i is a move which wins
-- directly (completes a line)
                       THEN win:=TRUE
                       ELSE posp:=pos; posp(i):=who;
-- examine the result of playing in this square
                            move(-who,posp,1,r);
```

137

```
-- -who is the opponent
                        win:= r=lose;
-- if he loses, we win

                IF r=draw
                THEN drawnmove:=i
-- keep a drawn move if possible
                FI
            FI
        FI
    DONE;
    IF win
    THEN place:=i; res:=win
    ELSE IF drawnmove=0
-- not even a draw is possible
            THEN res:=lose; i:=1;
-- play the first available square
                WHILE pos(i)<>0
                DO i:=i+1
                DONE;
                place:=i
            ELSE place:=drawnmove; res:=draw
-- keep the draw
            FI
        FI
    FI
ENDPROC move;
```

8) Another exercise for the reader, who should (we hope) try both programs on his own computer.

9) The following solution uses standard trial and error, backtracking when two queens can see each other. Better solutions exist, in particular by enumeration of the permutations of eight integers. The program given takes advantage of the fact that the eight queens must be in different columns, so that their x coordinates are fixed. The y coordinates are to be discovered.

```
ry: ARRAY (1..8) OF integer;    -- y coordinates of placed queens
np:=0; y:=0;   -- np number of queens placed
WHILE np<8
DO y:=y+1;      -- try next row
    IF y<9
    THEN IF free(np+1,y)
        THEN np:=np+1; ry(np):=y; y:=0    -- a queen on (np,y)
        FI;
    ELSE y:=ry(np); np:=np-1              -- backtrack
    FI
DONE

PROC free(i,j) RETURNS bool;
-- free  says whether the square (i,j) can be seen by a queen
```

```
-- already on the board (and thus in cols. 1 to i-1)
    k:=0; bad:=FALSE;
    WHILE k<i-1 AND NOT bad
-- for each queen already on the board
    DO k:=k+1;
        bad:= ry(k)=j OR pos(i-k)=pos(j-ry(k))
-- same row or same diagonal
    DONE;
    RETURN NOT bad
ENDPROC
```

Solutions to exercises on page 122

IN LISP

```
1. (DEFINE INVERSE
     (LAMDA (L1 L2)
        (COND
           (NULL(L1) L2)
           (T INVERSE(CDR(L1) CONS(CAR(L1) L2)))
    )))

2. (DEFINE INV1
     (LAMDA (L1 L2)
        (COND
           (NULL(L1) L2)
           (ATOM(CAR(L1)) INV1(CDR(L1) CONS(CAR(L1) L2)))
           (T INV1(CDR(L1) CONS(INV1(CAR(L1) NIL) L2))
    )))

3. (DEFINE ATOMISE
     (LAMDA (L1 L2)
        (COND
           (NULL(L1) L2)
           (ATOM(CAR(L1)) CONS(CAR(L1) ATOMISE(CDR(L1 L2)))
           (T ATOMISE(CAR(L1) ATOMISE(CDR(L1) L2))))
    )))
```

IN PROLOG

```
1. Solutions left to the reader.

2.
parent(x,y)->father(x,y);
parent(x,y)->mother(x,y);
grandparent(x,y)->parent(x,z) parent(z,y);
notfam(x,y)->mother(z,x) mother(v,y) dif(z,v);
first_cousin(x,y)->grandparent(z,x) grandparent(z,y) notpar(x,y);
```

This solution assumes that all families are stable, that is that marriages are unique, and that father and mother are always married. The number of rules becomes rapidly large when divorce and remarriage must be taken into account. The test is that of a shared grandparent and different mothers.

```
     To   test   the   program,   a family is defined by writing family
relationships such as:        .
mother(freda,michael);
father(eric,michael);
After creation of the family, the question
>first_cousin(x,y);
can be put. This prints out the complete list of first cousins.
```

An interesting point is the number of times the programs will output each pair of cousins. It is clear that the system considers (john,jean) and (jean,john) to be two independent pairs. The two examples of the same relation will thus be printed. Another exercise for the reader would be to produce such pairs only once.

The reader could perhaps introduce his own family tree to test the program.

3) The above family tree could also be used here.
4) Define first the list of people and jobs.
   Clauses 17 to 21 are written:

```
human(arthur)->;
human(bernard)->;
human(claude)->;
human(david)->;
human(eric)->;

and clauses 22-26:
job(musician)->;
job(navigator)->;
job(officer)->;
job(professor)->;
job(reporter)->;

     The constraints of the problem come from clauses 1-10:
activity(arthur,officer)->;
activity(bernard,professor)->;
activity(david,reporter)->;
not-activity(claude,musician)->;
not-activity(eric,officer)->;
not-activity(claude,officer)->;
not-activity(arthur,navigator)->;
not-activity(eric,professor)->;
not-activity(eric,navigator)->;
not-activity(bernard,officer)->;

     Constraints around family relationships come from clauses 11
to 15:
father(bernard,arthur)->;
father(david,claude)->;
father(eric,x)-> activity(x,professor);
grandfather(x,z)-> father(x,y)
                   father(y,z);
```

140

Note that we need the definition of grandfather.

```
profession(y,musician)-> activity(x,officier)
                         grandfather(y,x);

profession(y,navigator)-> activity(x,reporter)
                          father(x,y);
```

The following definitions describe relationships between functions:
```
not-profession(x,y)-> not-activity(x,y);
not-profession(x2,pl)-> activity(xl,pl)
                        human(x2)
                        dif(xl,x2);
not-profession(xl,p2)-> activity(xl,pl)
                        job(p2)
                        dif(pl,p2);
```

The program is activated by the command
>profession(x,y);

This leads to a list of the professions of the individuals concerned. Clauses 27 to 28 and 31 to 50 are not introduced, since, in PROLOG, predicates are not symmetrical (they are in fact relations) and there is thus no risk of confusion between a person and a profession. They are identified by their place in the relation. What is more, the inequality between individuals and professions is not required for each particular case, since there exists a predefined PROLOG predicate 'dif' which allows the expression of difference in general.

The statement
>not-profession(x,y);
allows the deduction of professions not exercised by individuals. Activating this clause leads to redundant replies, since there are several ways of obtaining them (clauses 52 to 51) and (clauses 1 to 10). Because of non-determinism, the PROLOG demonstrator will try all the possibilities, thus giving all the solutions.

5) Solutions are not given. We would be pleased to receive submissions.

Index

ADA 35
alpha-beta cutoff 48
analogy 100
ARCHES 100
artificial intelligence
  non-delivery of promised
  products 102
  present position 123-5
  specific languages for 24
  surveys 124
  techniques and tools in 23-4
  use of term 23
artificial systems, history and scope
  of 13-24
automatic picture analysis 21
automatic translation 14, 18
axiom sets 66

backgammon 16
backtracking 39, 44, 120
backward chaining 98, 99
Bernstein, Alex 15
binary graphs 31
  traversal of 32
binary matrix 33-5
binary trees 29
Boolean algebra 69

case enumeration 53
certitude degree 100
checkers 16
chess 14-17, 23, 26, 44-6, 48, 49
Chomsky, N. 19
clausal form 68, 80
combinatorial complexity 44, 45
combinatorial explosion 55-8
combinatorial problems 14

computer and the human brain 13
computer applications 15
conjunctive normal form 68

data structures 25-37
Davis-Putnam algorithm 71, 74
decision algorithm 13, 71
decision making 45, 91
decision tree 43, 46, 53, 55
  pruning 47-9
deduction path 101
deduction program 84
depth first search 44
draughts 16

electronic eye 19
elimination by theorems 51
Eliza 19
equivalent binary tree 30
evaluation 45-6, 57-8
existential quantifier 68
expert interface 94-5
expert systems 14, 18, 21-3, 89-104
  components of 89, 91-5
  current applications 101-2
  development needs 103
  function of 89
  future 102-4
  industrial products 101
  interfaces to 96
  present position 123-4
  research directions 99-1
  rules applied 97
  user interface 96-7
  users 95-6
  see also theorem provers

142

Achevé d'imprimer en janvier 1987 sur les presses de l'imprimerie Laballery
58500 Clamecy

Dépôt légal : janvier 1987

Numéro d'imprimeur : 612068